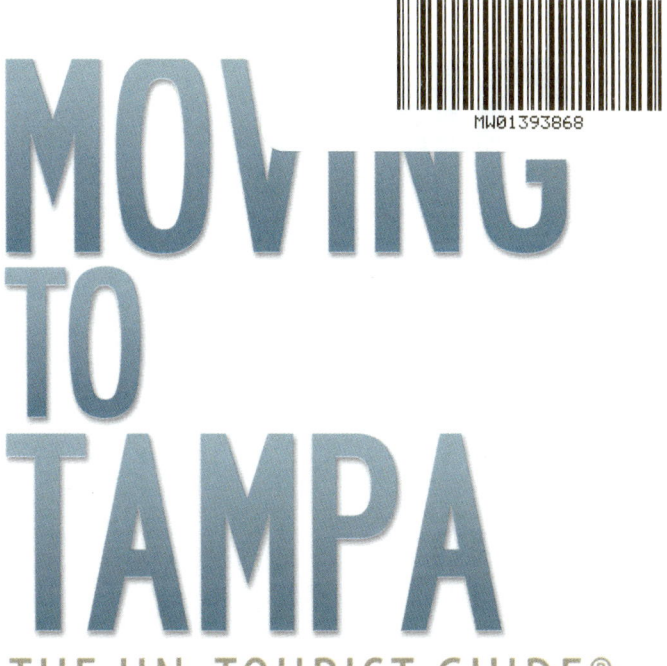

MOVING TO TAMPA

THE UN-TOURIST GUIDE®

SECOND EDITION

NEWT BARRETT

Copyright © 2016 by Newt Barrett

Published by Voyager Media, Inc.

All rights reserved. No part of this book may be reproduced in any manner whatsoever without written permission, except in the case of brief quotations embodied in critical articles and reviews.

Cover design and interior layout by www.PearCreative.ca

Printed in the U.S.A

Print: 978-0-9972461-5-5
eBook: ISBN: 978-0-9972461-6-2

CONTENTS

Foreword   7
Welcome to Tampa by Mayor Bob Buckhorn

Introduction   11
Tampa - Naturally Appealing, Incredibly Inviting
     Why Tampa?   14

Chapter 1   19
Background Check
     Brief History of Tampa   19
     Tampa Facts at a Glance   22

Chapter 2   24
Geographic and Community Guide to Tampa
     Getting to Know Hillsborough Communities   24
     Getting Around Town   30
     The Climate   32

Chapter 3   34
Choosing Where to Live in Tampa
     Cost of Housing   35
     Know Your Tampa Neighborhoods   36
     Up and Coming Communities and Developments   39
     East Hillsborough County   40
     Utilities   41
     Taxes   42
     Feeling Safe in Tampa?   43
     Healthcare and Medical Facilities   44

Chapter 4 — 49
Shopping
From Big Malls to Boutiques, Home Decor to Designer Fashions	49
Grocery & Gourmet Shopping	52
Major Shopping Malls	55
Shopping for Bargains and Good Causes	57
Filling You in on Fashion Finds	64

Chapter 5 — 67
Things to Do
Festivals	69
Sporting Life	70
Heart for the Arts	71
Culinary Arts	75
Spectacular Points of View	82
Perks of Parks	83
Area Attractions	84

Chapter 6 — 87
From Pre-K to Post Grad: Childcare and Education
Infant and Toddler Care	87
Tampa…with Tots	89
Public and Private Schools	92
After School Educational Activities	95
Higher Education: College and Beyond	97

Chapter 7 — 102
Our Diversified Economy
Doing Business in Tampa	102
Tampa Bay Economic Climate	106

Chapter 8 — 110
Fitting In and Finding Out
- Volunteer Opportunities — 111
- Local Media — 114

Chapter 9 — 119
On the Move to Tampa

Conclusion — 121

Valuable Resources and — 123

Sources of Information — 123

About the Author — 129

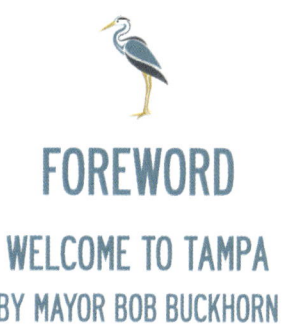

FOREWORD
WELCOME TO TAMPA
BY MAYOR BOB BUCKHORN

Tampa was built with the resilience and determination of immigrants from Cuba, Italy, Spain, South and Central Americas, Scotland and others. Tampa provided equal opportunity, prosperity, and safety to all who came, however what they brought to this city was just as valuable as what our city offered them. These people gave us a vision and brought their motivation to our city. They were able to lay the groundwork for a better tomorrow, a vision that our community is still building on today.

The Tampa that stands today is made up of the foundations of our early roots. Old cigar factories, once the staple and backbone of our city's economy, are still dispersed along our streets and the old Tampa Bay Hotel, built by railroad tycoon Henry B. Plant, still stands today as the University of Tampa.

Perseverance has led our journey from a small port town to the 53rd largest city in the United States. It's our attitude and vision that led us out of the Great Recession. While there was no clear cut path for our recovery, we came out stronger.

We are proud of the inclusive and accepting environment that this city emulates. Our diversity has propelled our creativity and innovation which has led to our economic competitiveness. This openness has laid foundation for Tampa to be competitive for trade, intellectual capital and business. Tampa is a city where an individual or family, no matter their race, religion, gender, or sexual orientation has the opportunity to prosper.

Tampa's renaissance is real. We are building communities that provide a true live, work and play environment. We are creating neighborhoods that foster public safety, healthy living, and highest quality of life. All areas of Tampa are transforming to benefit each resident even more than they have before. In downtown Tampa, we completed the Riverwalk, a project that was championed by 6 dedicated mayors and pushed through 40 years until its completion in 2015. The Hillsborough River, Tampa's most valuable natural asset, is featured on this waterside walkway and also connects our downtown in a new innovative way. In the Channel District, we are efficiently exporting goods and connecting with international markets. In West Tampa conceiving and developing neighborhoods that are safer, provide choices, and afford more residents the opportunity to raise a family. And soon Tampa will be home to the world's first WELL Certified district, a community with a modern focus on health and wellness, walkability, clean air, and sustainable development.

Tampa is a city that is transforming and growing with the people that inhabit it. We are becoming greater with your help and making people fall in love with Tampa all over again.

Welcome to Tampa.

Mayor Bob Buckhorn

INTRODUCTION
TAMPA-NATURALLY APPEALING, INCREDIBLY INVITING

Native American Indians, Spanish explorers and swashbuckling pirates were the first to discover the special charms of this city by the bay. What was a sparsely populated area primarily inhabited by palmettos, pines and scrubs, gradually grew from a modest port town into a major metropolitan area that still manages to exude the warmth and welcoming feel of a much smaller city.

Its waterfront, a landscape filled with lush, tropical foliage and the year-round sunshine and warm weather so typical of Florida, define the area's natural beauty.

Not just another pretty place, Tampa is a vibrant city boasting and hosting a world class, international airport, professional sports teams, high-end retail, fine dining experiences, multi-national companies, state-of-the-art medical facilities, colleges and universities, MacDill Air Force Base and so much more.

That's not to say it's all work and no play around these parts. Tampa knows how to throw a party, whether hosting a Super Bowl, welcoming the 2012 Republican National Convention or rolling out the red carpet for the International Indian Film Academy's so-called Bollywood Oscars awarded here in April 2014.

This Central Florida West Coast community is also an ideal place to start a career, start a family or start enjoying retirement. From the lofts located in Ybor City to the bungalows of Seminole Heights, and from the high-rise luxury condominiums lining Bayshore Boulevard to the gated communities of New Tampa, there are living spaces for all lifestyles.

Tampa also offers plenty of perks such as parks and playgrounds, museums and arts districts, golf courses and tennis courts, opera and orchestras and aquariums and zoos. Everything you need for a well-rounded lifestyle is available and easily accessible no matter where you reside in the Tampa area.

One of the most compelling reasons to make Tampa your new home is best summed up by Rick Homans, president and CEO of the Tampa Hillsborough Economic Development Corp.:

"Currently, the Tampa metropolitan area leads the state of Florida in job gains. In the past two years alone, more than 50 companies have selected Hillsborough County as the site of their relocation and expansion activities, generating over 8,700 new jobs and $688 million in capital investment. Global market leaders, including Bristol-Myers Squibb, Morgan Stanley, The Depository Trust & Clearing Corporation, Time Warner Business Services, USAA and Amazon have expressed their confidence in our community by announcing plans for significant, strategic growth."

Whatever your reason for moving here, you'll find our book a compelling guide chock full of insights and information to make you feel right at home.

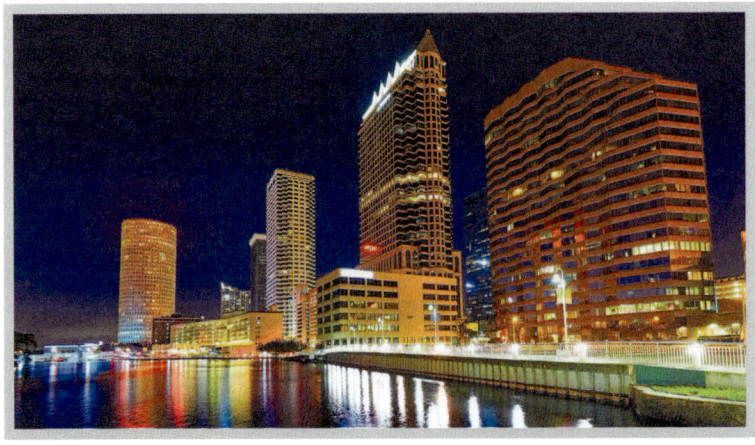

Tampa skyline at sunrise

A Few Fun Facts

For newcomers, former residents who may be returning to their roots or anyone who needs to get quickly up to speed about Tampa, there are a few things you need to know.

- You are not living in Tampa Bay. That term is loosely used by news crews and sportscasters who don't understand that it is a regional reference and not a specific city. Tampa Bay is a body of water; the Tampa Bay area covers Tampa, St. Petersburg, Clearwater and the beaches.

- Native or newcomer, while living in Tampa, you are likely to be referred to as either a Tampanian or a Tampan.

- Nicknames for your new hometown include Cigar City, The Big Guava, Lightning Capital of the World and Cigar Capital of the World. Tampa was known worldwide for its hand-rolled cigars.

- Native American Indians are believed to have named this area Tanpa, a word thought to mean "Sticks of Fire," inspired by its frequent lightning storms.

- The sidewalk that parallels Bayshore Boulevard is thought to be the longest continuous sidewalk in the world at 4.5 miles long. It's a terrific place to run, walk, bicycle, or get active in any way with views of Hillsborough Bay and downtown Tampa.

- Tampa and St. Petersburg were the first two cities in the world to have regularly scheduled passenger airline service.

- Tampa's sister cities include Agrigento, Italy; Ashdod, Israel; Barranquilla, Colombia; Izmir, Turkey; LeHavre, France; Oviedo, Spain; Porto Alegre, Brazil; South Dublin County, Ireland; and Vera Cruz, Mexico.

- Legendary musician Ray Charles began his career as a teenager playing dance halls in Tampa in 1946.

- Before his performance on "The Ed Sullivan Show" in 1956, Elvis Presley played one of his first concerts at Tampa's Ft. Homer Hesterly Armory.

- The Civil War steamship *Scottish Chief* was found in the Hillsborough River in August 2009, after having sunk more than 140 years prior.

- And Big Guava? Steve Otto, a *Tampa Tribune* newspaper columnist, insisted if New York could be the Big Apple it was only right Tampa's claim to fame should be guavas.

- Every year the city is invaded by hundreds of pirates, in elaborate costume and make-up, who arrive aboard a fully rigged pirate ship, not in search of treasure but simply for pleasure. Gasparilla has been a Tampa tradition since the early 1900s and locals plan pirate-themed parties that stretch from early morning until late night. Eye patches and talking like a pirate, that day in particular, are encouraged.

Why Tampa?

Ten Reasons to Live in Tampa (In No Particular Order)

1. **Natural Beauty.** Lush foliage, sparkling waterfronts and nightly displays of colorful sunsets are just part of the allure of this West Coast community. Tall palm trees add a tropical touch, bays, lakes, rivers and other bodies of water are in abundance and a year 'round growing season means something's always in bloom.

2. **Wonderful Weather.** This Central Florida, west coast community typically boasts temperatures and clear skies that make it possible to enjoy outdoor activities year-round. That means playing golf and tennis, going fishing and boating or enjoying cycling and running with only a slight seasonal adjustment of outdoor attire.

Sunset on Tampa Bay

3. **Excellent Entertainment.** The range of world-class performers who make appearances here throughout the year is an impressive list that includes top opera singers to rock stars, touring productions of hit Broadway shows to professional dance companies and classical musicians to kings and queens of comedy.

Historic Tampa Theatre is one of the many venues that bring world class entertainment to the city

4. **Casual Lifestyle.** Although black tie galas and lots of elegant events frequently crowd social calendars, for the most part, the day-to-day dress code is more relaxed than restrained. The look can be tropical cool, neatly chic or very vintage but the key is dressing for comfort and climate.

5. **Spectacular Sports.** Fans have a lot to cheer about whether it is for professional sports like NFL Football's the Tampa Bay Buccaneers, Major League Baseball's the Tampa Bay Rays, the National Hockey League's Tampa Bay Lightning, spring training when the New York Yankees are on deck at Steinbrenner Field or the North American Soccer League's Tampa Bay Rowdies. Annual sports events include two leading teams competing in college football's Outback Bowl and the high-speed action of the Firestone Grand Prix IndyCar series race across the streets of St. Petersburg.

6. **Great Outdoors.** Tampa offers everything from private golf courses to public parks, offshore to deep-sea fishing, canoe and kayak excursions to stand up paddle boarding, hiking and biking to running and sunning.

Sunrise to sunset enjoy year round recreational activities in Tampa

7. **Wild to Mild.** Our city boasts many great ways to observe all sorts of native to non-native creatures. We are a top bird migratory and watching spot as well as a great place to be entertained by manatees and dolphins moving along the waterfront. Major attractions like Busch Gardens Tampa Bay, Lowry Park Zoo and the Florida Aquarium deliver all sorts of wildlife encounters while Big Cat Rescue serves as a sanctuary for rescued, rehabilitating and endangered species of big cats.

8. **Multi-cultural, multi-ethnic.** Tampa is a melting pot that welcomes people from around the world and all sorts of cultural influences. This rich diversity is recognized during annual festivals, special events and parades and featured at ethnic restaurants. Tampa is also is the home to the nation's only tri-lingual newspaper, *La Gaceta*, which is published in English, Spanish and Italian.

Tampa Union Station welcomes train passengers traveling on AMTRAK

9. **Great Gateway.** With its world-class airport, lively cruise ship terminal, cross-country AMTRAK railroad service and major interstate highway connections, Tampa is perfect for locals who travel for work or for pleasure. Whether traveling by air, water or land, these connectors make it easy to go anywhere in the world.

10. **Urban to Suburban.** Looking for a loft in the city center or longing for a piece of land where you can plant a garden? Want to restore a bungalow back to its original beauty or need a deluxe home complete with its own dock? Then Tampa's got a spot for you. Select from historic neighborhoods to condos overlooking the Port of Tampa. Opt for a waterfront view from a colonial-style Bayshore mansion or go for the gusto of living adjacent to a private golf course.

CHAPTER 1
BACKGROUND CHECK

Brief History of Tampa

Tampa's transformation from a small, swampy, barely-there village to a major, multi-cultural metropolis owes a great deal to a colorful cast of characters who helped shape this city's fortunes and future.

First to call this Central Florida West Coast area home were Native American Indians likely drawn by the abundance of game, a semi-tropical climate, fertile soil and a waterfront brimming with fish. It is believed Caloosa Indians dubbed the village they inhabited Tanpa, a word meaning "sticks of fire," possibly inspired by the dramatic lightning displays that light up the sky. However, when the name was recorded, it was officially written as Tampa.

European explorers later followed, making their way into Tampa Bay, coming ashore and trekking into the Florida wilderness, many driven by a desire to find gold while others began life in a new land.

Eventually other settlers followed as Tampa transitioned into an area teeming with troops, traders and pioneers drawn by the area's lively port and military fort. It officially became a U.S. territory in 1845.

By the late 1800s, a railroad baron named Henry B. Plant greatly impacted the area's growth when he extended his rail system here, creating a vital link for travelers and trade. Over the next few years, the city's population reportedly exploded from several hundred to more than 3,000.

A bridge across the Hillsborough River proved to be key not only to connecting the downtown district with the rest of the city but also to prompting Plant to build a lavish resort on the west banks of the river. The Tampa Bay Hotel opened to great fanfare in 1891, welcoming visitors who flocked here to enjoy Florida's warm, winter weather as well as celebrities, athletes and politicians who graced its grounds over the years. The original building still stands with its signature silver minarets creating a striking silhouette against the downtown skyline. No longer a hotel, the building is now home to the University of Tampa.

The former Tampa Bay Hotel is now the University of Tampa

Meanwhile, just east of downtown, Vicente Martinez Ybor was purchasing land and building the first of many factories that produced hand-rolled cigars. The industry would eventually employ nearly 12,000 workers and bring what became known as Ybor City global fame as the "Cigar Capital of the World."

When the combined impact of mechanization, the rising popularity of cigarettes and the Depression decimated the labor-intensive industry, many of the immigrants who worked in the factories found new livelihoods and stayed. Generations later, their descendants continue to enrich the diversity and cultural heritage that is a vital characteristic of this area.

Ybor City is a designated National Historic Landmark District

Waterways have always played a role in Tampa's past, from the time pirates plied its coast until shiploads of phosphate set sail from its docks. Port Tampa continues to fuel economic development as cargo ships and passenger cruise lines continuously drop anchor at its terminals, generating enough activity and revenue to rank this among the nation's largest ports.

Aviation has also been critical to boosting Tampa's profile for commerce and travel, both nationally as well as internationally. Tampa Bay's milestone contribution to aviation history dates back to 1914, when the world's first scheduled commercial airline service was successfully launched by the St. Petersburg-Tampa Airboat Line and piloted by Tony Jannus.

No history of Tampa would be complete without mention of its military presence and personnel. When the U.S. declared war on Spain in 1898, Tampa was the port of embarkation for troops headed to Cuba. And it was here that a colorful colonel named Theodore (Teddy) Roosevelt organized the first volunteer cavalry in the Spanish-American War, the "Rough Riders."

Because of its strategic location during that war, Tampa was selected as the site where troops gathered before shipping off for Cuba. A camp established to accommodate the thousands of personnel amassed here was located in what was then known as Port Tampa City. That former encampment now borders what has become a major military installation, MacDill Air Force Base.

MacDill Air Force Base, an active U.S. Air Force base, was officially activated in 1941

MacDill Air Force Base, perched on the southwestern tip of Tampa, is also headquarters for U.S. Central Command (USCENTCOM) and U.S. Special Operations Command (USSOCOM).

Today, Tampa is far from a fishing village. The city and its surrounding communities represent a diverse mix of industries that include agriculture, tourism, technology, health care, financial services and transportation.

Tampa remains an area of growth and opportunity and retains many of the original features that first attracted inhabitants to its shore.

Tampa Facts at a Glance

- Largest city in Hillsborough County and the county seat
- Third most populous city in Florida.
- About one-third of the population of Hillsborough County lives in Tampa

- Economic base includes tourism, agriculture, construction, finance, health care, government, technology and Port of Tampa.

Source: City of Tampa (www.tampagov.net)

Tampa Bay

- Metropolitan area comprised of Tampa-St. Petersburg-Clearwater

- Four-county area is composed of nearly 2.9 million residents

- Ranks as second largest metropolitan statistical area (MS) in Florida and fourth largest in the Southeastern U.S.

Source: Wikipedia: http://en.wikipedia.org/wiki/Tampa,_Florida

City of Tampa postcard mural

CHAPTER 2
GEOGRAPHIC AND COMMUNITY GUIDE TO TAMPA

Located midway along Central Florida's West Coast, Tampa's central location is primarily a low-lying and plateau-like area, similar to much of the state's landscape. The predominantly sea level city is bordered by Old Tampa Bay and Hillsborough Bay, large bodies of water that unite to form Tampa Bay which feeds into the Gulf of Mexico.

The Hillsborough River is the primary source of freshwater for this area. It flows from the north before passing through downtown Tampa and eventually emptying into Hillsborough Bay.

Getting to Know Hillsborough Communities

Tampa is the largest of three incorporated cities in Hillsborough County as well as the county seat.

Spanning 1,020 square miles of land and 24 miles of inland water area, Hillsborough ranked as Florida's fourth most populated county in 2012, tallying an estimated 1.28 million people, according to the U.S. Census Bureau.

Tampa's population equaled 347,645 in 2012, with the remaining two incorporated areas, Plant City and Temple Terrace, contributing an additional 35,903 and 25,189 residents, respectively.

Geographic and Community Guide to Tampa

See detailed Google Map version online:
www.google.com/maps/@28.0247907,-82.4686195,11z

Government offices and professional firms fill downtown Tampa and the Westshore area boasts the highest concentration of office space (4,000 businesses and more than 93,000 employees) in Florida. But, both areas boast growing residential bases and throughout Tampa there are multiple housing options, ranging from quiet neighborhoods to industrial-looking lofts.

Among the oldest neighborhoods are Hyde Park and Seminole Heights, formerly forlorn areas that have been, or are being, lovingly restored, revitalized and reinvigorated and now boast award-winning architecture and well maintained lawns.

Residents, who want to be close to the water as well as to downtown Tampa, can become island-dwellers by living on either Harbour Island or Davis Islands.

An aerial view of Davis Islands and the downtown Tampa waterfront

Harbour Island is a more recent mixed-used development dominated by luxury homes, high-rise offices and a high-end hotel.

Just across the channel is Davis Islands, a collection of islands with homes ranging from modest to mansions, as well as Peter O'Knight Airport, primarily used for private planes and flight instruction, and one of the area's leading medical facilities, Tampa General Hospital.

Areas like Ybor City and West Tampa remain vital links to Tampa's past. They have been predominantly influenced by Hispanic, Cuban, and Italian populations for generations and are distinguished by red brick streets and former cigar factories refurbished into offices and artists' studios.

Some of the city's most stately homes are nestled along the tree-lined, scenic streets of Ballast Point, Palma Ceia, and the waterfront bordered by Bayshore Boulevard. Many of the city's prominent politicians and business leaders have either grown up or raised families of their own here.

One of the newer and more noticeable residential areas, with its concentration of high rise residential towers, is the Channel District that offers views of Tampa's working port and the downtown skyline.

The Channel District features towers of condos and apartment in an urban setting

Because most of the city's most central areas are already heavily populated and densely developed, growth has been forced to spread to the north and east. Areas where there once were more farms than families and citrus groves than grocery stores are now filled with single-family homes, retail centers and multi-lane thoroughfares.

Ever-expanding unincorporated areas like Carrollwood remain popular spots for families and businesses. Likewise, eastward to Brandon, vibrant commercial and residential development continues while new subdivisions in Westchase, Tampa Palms and New Tampa help accommodate the area's on-going growth as more and more people are attracted by the affordability and affability of these areas.

Why Tampa Bay?

People choose places to live for many different reasons, but for me, the airport in Tampa was quite an important factor when I moved here from England 24 years ago. For anyone who travels, the airport is very well planned, and it's usually possible to be driving out in a car within 15 minutes of landing. Because it's close to the city, the airport is also only 15-20 minutes from some of the best residential areas in Tampa Bay.

Maddy Krasne

The lifestyle choices offered here are abundant. There are high-end condominiums and large mansions lining Bayshore Boulevard offering million-dollar views of the waterfront that are also close to the downtown business district and the many amenities of South Tampa.

There are great restaurants, good sports facilities and, of course, the proximity to water is great for boat lovers. The Tampa Bay area has waterfront homes with open bay views and, on the west side of the peninsula, there are canals with easy access to the bay. Marinas and membership-based yacht clubs are conveniently located on Davis Islands, Harbour Island and in the Ballast Point area of South Tampa so if your home does not include private docking facilities, you can still enjoy find a nearby spot for your sailboat, powerboat or yacht.

For those who prefer a gated community near downtown, Harbour Island offers security, a manicured landscape, waterfront homes, plus the convenience of Harbour Island Athletic Club, which has tennis courts, an outdoor pool and extensive gym facilities.

The local weather is one of the major influences for anyone who enjoys outdoor activities. The warm, sunny, clear days of our winters, coupled with an average daytime temperature around 70 degrees, makes it possible to enjoy the outdoors for most of the year. Activities such as sailing, paddle-boarding and canoeing are all available in many places. South Tampa boasts two yacht clubs, the Tampa Yacht Club and the Davis Island Yacht Club, both of which have an active membership and social facilities.

It's not all about the water, either. For golf lovers, there are excellent tournament courses plus several golf resorts in the vicinity, some offering high-end homes around the perimeter. The northern areas of the city, like Avila, Hunter's Green and Tampa Palms, also offer some beautiful gated communities with larger homes and large lots, for those wanting acreage and more privacy.

For families, school districts are important, and those with young children favor the shaded, tree-lined streets of South Tampa's Hyde Park historic district. Old Hyde Park Village provides a pleasant stroll around its smaller shops and restaurants and is also a great location for art festivals, Sunday markets and outdoor jazz nights. In terms of amenities, the arts are not forgotten, with a major focus being the downtown area.

The Performing Arts Center (known as the Straz Center) contains several theaters and houses major musical productions, plays and some fringe activities. The Tampa Museum of Art is close by, and is constantly changing its offerings. The downtown area is enhanced by the Hillsborough River, which forms its western border, another pleasant feature of the city.

The homes in Tampa Bay are also quite varied in style. In many cases, older, single-story homes have been replaced by modern, elevated homes, often with Mediterranean styling, although some custom homes are very individual.

There's also the pleasant community of Davis Islands with its wide streets and eclectic atmosphere, which is where I live. Charming and quirky are some of the adjectives that describe what once was a pile of silt and is now home to around 5,000 people. The short stretch of East Davis Boulevard has the feel of a busy, small village center. It's close to major highways, convenient for getting around, surrounded by water and naturally beautiful, ideal for biking, walking or running and perfect for walks with my Labrador.

And it has one of the few real beaches in Tampa, which makes this ideal for water-oriented sports like paddle-boarding.

The weather also allows semi-tropical landscaping, so that palm trees and large flowering vegetation such as hibiscus and bougainvillea add a relaxed beauty to the environment.

So whatever is most important to you, it's highly likely that this city can offer a rewarding place to live. Come and see!

MADELEINE KRASNE CLHMS
Broker Associate
Premier Sotheby's International Reality
www.sothebysrealty.com

Getting Around Town

What is commonly referred to as the Tampa Bay area is comprised of Tampa, St. Petersburg and Clearwater and boasts a combined population base representing some 2.9 million residents.

Residents of both Hillsborough and Pinellas counties commonly commute between both areas, with students, professionals and part-time workers opting to live on one side of Tampa Bay while attending college or finding employment on the opposite side of the bay.

Beautiful waterfront views are one of this area's many natural amenities but those are limited to bays, lakes and rivers. A direct view of the

Geographic and Community Guide to Tampa

Gulf of Mexico requires a drive over to neighboring Pinellas County, home of both St. Petersburg and Clearwater.

Tampa is a city that primarily requires a vehicle for ease, quickness and comfort of getting around. Taxis and buses are options but our community is so spread out that those can quickly become pricey and time-consuming.

The area's leading high-speed, heavy volume roadways are I-275 and I-75 that serve as the major north-south thoroughfares. Both connect with I-4 which is a heavily used highway continuing through Orlando to Florida's east coast.

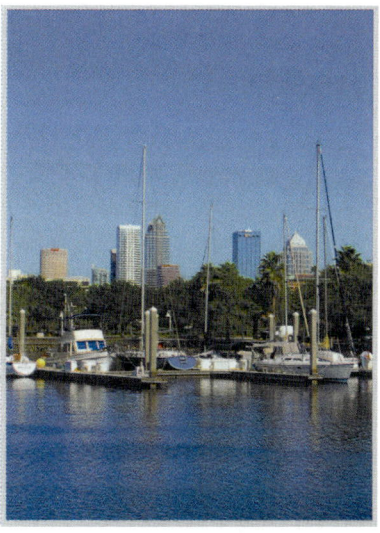
Residents can easily access the waterfront from areas throughout Tampa

Without any major mass transportation options in the near future, traffic and parking are issues just about anywhere in the city and at any time of day or night.

Only downtown Tampa offers an option of riding either the rubber-tired In-Town Trolley or electric TECO Line Streetcar that moves multiple passengers around within a limited area for a fee.

Electric vehicle charging stations are slowly spreading throughout the city offering those with a plug-in vehicle an option to park and charge for a fee.

Sources: Tampa By the Numbers

www.census.gov/quickfacts/table/PST045215/1271000,00

www.city-data.com/city/Tampa-Florida.html

31

Moving to Tampa

TECO Line Streetcar connects Ybor City and the Channel District with downtown Tampa

The Climate

Fortunately, waterways tend to offer some relief from Florida heat. Bay breezes deliver a cooling touch that makes summertime highs hovering near, or into, the 90s a bit more bearable. Tampa's temperate, semi-tropical climate does not necessarily end with the onset of fall or even winter. Warm weather tends to linger here long after it has abandoned other areas of the country.

When temperatures do eventually drop, the contrast creates a welcome briskness and adds a slight brace to the air.

The area's normally placid waterfronts can become turbulent during tropical storms and hurricanes. Waterspouts have become increasingly common during summer months, creating dramatic glimpses of tall, dark spirals that can be a real distraction to drivers crossing bridges and a danger to nearby boaters. When sufficient rain coincides with high tides, that combination can create flood conditions that may make some roads un-passable or even result in mandatory evacuations.

Heat and humidity are noticeable throughout much of the year while winters tend to be a bit more mild and marked by drier conditions. Occasional freezes have been recorded but winter temperatures typically hover around the 50-degree mark.

Hurricane season is generally defined as June through November but sometimes Mother Nature makes her own timeline. Historically there have been severe hurricanes that have created widespread devastation but nothing of that magnitude has hit the Tampa Bay area lately. There have been no major hurricanes or direct hits here since 1921 but there have been plenty of major storms and close calls. The most recent rash of hard-hitting weather was in 2004. The 2013 Atlantic hurricane season was the least harrowing in 30 years.

Still, hurricanes are a fact of life and preparation can be key to survival. Residents are accustomed to going through a hurricane preparedness checklist every year and an increasing number of households now have generators in case electric power is lost for long periods of time.

Basics may include knowing where to move your car to higher ground if you live in a flood prone area. If you have a four-legged friend, stock up on pet food as well as people food and have an evacuation destination in mind that welcomes pets. Make sure medical supplies and first aid kits are well stocked and prescriptions are current.

Be sure to know your evacuation routes and shelter locations in advance.

Because power failures may kill your ATM and close your gas station, keep a supply of cash handy all season long and don't leave filling your car's gas tank until the last minute.

Hillsborough County officials recommend having enough supplies on hand to last at least three days. That includes food that does not require cooking or refrigeration, plenty of water for drinking and flashlights with extra batteries.

Most important, mandatory evacuations need to be heeded. While hurricanes are unpredictable it is always important to remember to protect yourself and loved ones. Homes and businesses can be repaired or replaced.

CHAPTER 3
CHOOSING WHERE TO LIVE IN TAMPA

Tampa is literally a city for all ages and all phases of life. The housing mix ranges from apartment buildings to town homes, single-family bungalows to urban lofts and grand mansions to luxury penthouses.

Whether beginning a career or enjoying your retirement, there are areas that may be more suited to your lifestyle and more appropriate for your particular interests than others.

SoHo, a residential and commercial area named for its South Howard location, is well known for pub crawls, happy hour specials and nightlife while Sun City Center, which is found south of Tampa, is an age-restricted community where active seniors live and are known to commute short distances by golf cart.

Tampa is, above all, a welcoming community that strives to be a good neighbor to all. Families, retirees, young professionals and same sex couples can be found living, working and enjoying leisure time activities throughout the city and its surrounding communities.

While dwelling on just where to find your dwelling, keep in mind that options are plentiful. Want to be immersed in an urban setting, prefer a more "green" vantage point from a home overlooking a manicured golf course, love to be surrounded by history or want to cast your gaze on the sparkling waterfront and bustling Port Tampa Bay? Then you're in the right place.

Cost of Housing

Here are some representative prices of various sizes and styles of housing in the Tampa, Florida area.

$485,000 - Downtown Tampa: 2 BR/2 B 17th floor 1157 sq. ft. condo
$1.29M - Hyde Park: 4BR/5B 3189 sq. ft. single family
$528,000 - New Tampa: 6BR/4B 5510 sq. ft. single family
$875,000 - Culbreath Isles: 3BR/2.5B 2431 sq. ft. canal front single family
$379,000 - Seminole Heights: Classic 1926 3BR/2.5B 2698 sq. ft. home
$366,000 - Apollo Beach: 3BR/2B 1840 sq. ft. waterfront ranch with pool
$323,757 - Westchase: 4BR/4B 2600 sq. ft. single family home
$174,900 - Carrollwood Village—3BR/2.5B 1497 sq. ft. single family
Source: Zillow.com

Happily, most neighborhoods in the Tampa area provide a broad range of housing options from very affordable to very expensive. Thus, you are likely to find just the right home in a wide range of neighborhoods.

Compare Tampa options to what you can buy around the country:

- $799,000 - A one-bedroom 1195 sq. ft. condo in downtown Boston

- $1,400,000 - A 1940s three-bedroom home in Los Angeles

- $1,000,000 - two-bedroom 1155 sq. ft. condo, Hoboken, New Jersey

- $1,094,000- A two-bedroom condo in Arlington, VA, nearWashington, D.C

- $449,000—A newly constructed single-family home in Houston, Texas

- $599,900—A two-bedroom condo in downtown Minneapolis

- $1,799,000—A three-bedroom,four-bath condo in Glen Cove,Long Island, New York

Know Your Tampa Neighborhoods

Here is a breakdown of some of the signature Tampa neighborhoods and a gauge of what types of rental rates and sales prices you could encounter.

For a snapshot of what areas are hot and what prices those listings are generating, check out the Tampa Real Estate Overview on Trulia. Here is an example of the information it provides:

Market trends help you understand the movement of key price indicators. Trends in Tampa show a 8% year-over-year rise in median sales price and a 3% rise in median rent per month.

The median sales price for homes in Tampa for May 4 to Aug 3, 2016 was $203,050 based on 564 home sales. Average price per square foot for Tampa was $139, an increase of 14% compared to the same period last year.

A comprehensive overview of the average listing price sales price and price per square foot can be found on Trulia's Tampa Home Prices page.

Rental rates for homes and apartments vary widely based on location, square footage and amenities. For insights into the area's inventory and price points for housing rentals, check out Tampa Houses for Rent on Zillow.com. And visit Zillow.com for Tampa Apartment Rentals information.

Downtown Tampa offers an increasingly vibrant mix of apartments and condos, rentals and sales. This area is perfect for people who work downtown and love the idea of walking to their workplace or those who are patrons of the arts or sports fans and are happy to stroll to the performing arts center, hockey arena or whatever concert, festival or special event is happening downtown. There are select retail establishments nearby. Duckweed Urban Market, billed as Downtown Tampa's Neighborhood Grocery Store, features ready-to-eat meals, craft beers, pet food and basics like locally roasted ground coffees and freshly baked goods.

Duckweed Urban Market is the neighborhood grocery for Tampa's downtown.

Historic neighborhoods like <u>Hyde Park</u>, east of downtown, and <u>Seminole Heights</u>, centrally located just north of the downtown district, are considered desirable places to live for their looks and lifestyle. Tree-lined streets, front porches, well-cared-for lawns and tastefully restored or renovated homes—from elegant Southern Colonial architecture to quaint Craftsman-style bungalows—are the norm for these highly residential areas. Both areas have undergone resurgences but Hyde Park is considered to be the more polished and prestigious address while Seminole Heights is viewed as a more eclectic, artsy area in terms of its residents and aesthetic.

Harbour Island and Davis Islands are large land masses that were created by dredging. Both boast an abundance of waterfront, offer rentals as well as condominiums and single-family residences and provide residents with convenient locations to the downtown area as well as easy access to major east-west and north-south connectors. Harbour Island had little more than a phosphate terminal on its land until the 80s when a developer added commercial ventures like office space, a hotel and restaurants. Residential development now dominates the island and prices are at a premium. Davis Islands offers quite a range of possibilities from stately homes to historical buildings that offer apartments, to modest duplexes, from traditional to contemporary single-family homes and even a mansion owned by New York Yankees professional baseball player Derek Jeter.

Originally developed in the 1960s, Culbreath Isles was one of the first gated, waterfront communities established in Tampa. It remains one of the few private enclaves of its kind in South Tampa. Lovely homes have gradually been supplanted by ever more luxurious mansions that propel prices to the million-dollar-plus level. This area is a real draw for those who like to dock their yachts and sailboats close to home. Residents are within minutes of Tampa International Airport, are conveniently close to upscale dining and shopping and are considered to live in one of the area's most desirable school districts.

An established Tampa neighborhood that dates back to the late 1800s, Carrollwood was flush with citrus groves and cattle ranches for decades. From that former pastoral scene has emerged a heavily populated, highly developed community that is well served by major highways and nearby interstate corridors. You will find family-oriented neighborhoods with an abundance of medical and health care treatment centers here. Traffic can be challenging depending on the time of day and what direction drivers are headed but the multi-lanes and relatively high speed of the main thoroughfare, North Dale Mabry Highway, keeps things moving.

As growth and development continues to spread north, some of Tampa's newest residential areas are attracting families who seek spacious homes, gated communities and all of the amenities wanted within a convenient, well defined area. New Tampa is one of the largest residential areas in the city and is defined by its master-planned communities, like Cory Lake Isles, that feature modern homes and well groomed yards. Cory Lake Isles, one of Tampa's largest lake communities, is built around a 165-acre lake that is ideal for boating and water sports and boasts a 1,700-square-foot conservation preserve. Residents enjoy community pools, tennis courts, golf courses and jogging paths plus nearby major retailers, leading restaurants and trendy shops and boutiques.

Up and Coming Communities and Developments

Whether you are eager to locate your new home right away or opt to temporarily rent before selecting your new neighborhood, you may want to keep in mind the following projects and developments on the horizon:

ENCORE! ® expanded its resident-ready offerings from the first phase that opened in 2013. The Ella at ENCORE! is a mid-rise apartment building specifically suited for active seniors. Additional apartments will welcome singles, couples and families in 2014. The master-planned, mixed-use project is a private and public partnership that will create a vibrant community in an area bordering the downtown Tampa business district. When complete, the 40-acre, 12-block, energy-efficient retail, residential, cultural and recreational project will be home to 2,500 people.

Residences at the Riverwalk is a 36-story apartment building that will add 360 units to the downtown Tampa housing mix. It will rise north of Kennedy Boulevard, near the Straz Center for the Performing Arts.

SkyHouse Channelside is a 23-story, 320-unit rental apartment building that joins a number of residential towers already located in the Channel District that is bordered by downtown Tampa and Ybor City.

East Hillsborough will be the scene of significant commercial construction as work gets under way on a new 140,000-square-foot Bass Pro Shop in Brandon and an Amazon warehouse fulfillment center to be built in Riverview. Jobs generated by both projects will likely spur housing demand in and, in turn, more residential development in those areas as well.

The ENCORE is a master-planned community that provides rental properties for singles, couples, families and seniors.

East Hillsborough County

East Hillsborough County includes the communities of Riverview, Valrico, Apollo Beach, Ruskin, Plant City, and Lithia. An excellent highway system enables a quick commute into downtown Tampa.

Among the benefits of living in East Hillsborough County:

- Family-friendly towns with great schools

- An excellent healthcare facility: Brandon Regional Hospital

- A terrific 200 store shopping center, Westfield Brandon that hosts Macy's, Dillards, and lots of specialty shops from Apple to Michael Kors

- Convenient to many highways and to central Florida

- Just an hour from Gulf beaches

Utilities

City of Tampa residents receive a consolidated bill for three services: water, wastewater (sewer) and solid waste (refuse and recycling). More than 140,000 water meters located within a 211-square-mile service area measure monthly consumption levels.

Hillsborough County's Public Utility Department provides drinking water, wastewater treatment and disposal, solid waste collection and disposal and recycling services for residents in the unincorporated areas outside of the city limits. Tampa, Plant City and Temple Terrace are not part of the county's service area.

A rate schedule downloadable document for those various county services shows that a typical single-family home uses about 300 gallons of water daily. An online water bill calculator estimates that the monthly cost based on that usage is $27.94. That includes a $4.31 per 1,000 gallon wastewater charge that is capped at 8,000 gallons per month for each single-family home. County residents are provided with two garbage pickups, one recycling pickup and one yard waste pickup each week.

Fees for county trash collection and disposal services are billed annually. In 2014, single family homes located in unincorporated areas paid $222.75 for service from January through December.

TECO, Tampa Electric, has been the area's primary source of electric power since 1899. The current service area covers 2,000 square miles within the West Central Florida area that is inhabited by more than one million people.

As of January 2016, average TECO residential monthly bills for 1,000 kilowatt-hours decreased by $2.25 a month, or 5.5 percent, to $106.00 from the previous average of $108.25.

An Energy & Sustainability Report by Hillsborough County Government estimates an average family of four uses about 600 kilowatt hours of electricity per month, primarily for heating and cooling.

TECO contends its electric bills are 12% below the national average.

TECO People's Gas has provided Central Florida homes and business with natural gas for more than 117 years. Its residential rates averaged $41.53 per household.

For wireless and landline phones, cable TV and internet service, the area's primary providers are Bright House Networks and Verizon.

Bright House is the nation's 6th largest owner and operator of cable systems and the second largest in Florida. Customers may subscribe to one, or more, of the following: video, high-speed data and phone services. Headquartered in New York, Verizon Communications Inc., operates the largest 4G LTE network in the nation and global service to more than 150 countries.

Taxes

There is no personal income tax in Florida. But you will pay a range of other taxes, depending on where you live and whether you conduct business here. Below is a breakdown of the major taxes compiled by the State of Florida:

- Sales tax rate is 6%.

- Corporations that do business and earn income in Florida must file a corporate income tax return (unless they are exempt).

- Florida Property Tax is based on market value as of Jan. 1st that year.

Counties have the discretion to levy local taxes in addition to those that the state collects. Hillsborough County is among those levying a local sales tax. The 7% sales tax collected by Hillsborough County is equal to the average for all 67 Florida counties.

Property taxes are assessed and collected by the Hillsborough County Property Appraiser. There is an online tax estimator that enables you to figure out what the annual tax will be on a property based on an average millage (tax) rate of 21 mills or $21 per thousand. For example, a Tampa home with a market value of $100,000 that qualified for the homestead exemption, may be assessed $1,087-$1,278.

The site cautions that the "estimate does not include non-ad valorem taxes that may be applicable to this property, such as assessments for roads, fire, garbage, lighting, drainage, water, sewer, or homeowner association fees."

The State of Florida allows everyone who owns and resides on real property that is their permanent residence as of Jan. 1 to receive a homestead exemption up to $50,000. The first $25,000 applies to all property taxes, including school district taxes. The additional $25,000 applies to the assessed value between $50,000-$75,000 and only to non-school taxes. Homeowners must apply for exemptions through their county property appraiser. The application is Form DR-501 and forms can be downloaded.

First-time filers will need to answer the following:

- Whose name or names were recorded on the title on Jan. 1?
- What is the street address of the property?
- Were you living in the dwelling on Jan. 1?
- Do you claim homestead in another county or state?

Feeling Safe in Tampa?

No city is immune from crime but Tampa seems to be successfully monitoring public areas and taking measures to better maintain security for residents and visitors alike.

Tampa's increasingly vibrant economy, retiree population and popularity as a travel destination can make it an attractive target for scam artists, thieves on the lookout for valuables left unguarded in cars, muggings and even more violent crimes. But the city seems to be following a statewide trend and managing to keep crime on the decline.

A forceful show of law enforcement personnel and resources utilized during the 2012 Republican National Convention held in Tampa provided local law enforcement with surveillance cameras strategically placed throughout the downtown area. Those cameras may be contributing to making the city safer by monitoring criminal activity and even identifying individuals suspected of committing crimes.

To look up criminal activity within a particular area of Tampa, the City of Tampa web site links to a crime mapping resource called RAIDS Online. Residents outside of the city can access information about what crimes occur and where they happen through the Hillsborough County Sheriff's Office internet-based crime information and mapping link.

For a breakdown of the types of crime that most commonly occur within the city and the county, the Hillsborough Community Atlas provides annual crime statistics.

The chances of becoming a victim of a violent crime in Tampa are just 1 in 161, slightly more than for Florida, which shows a 1 in 205 chance.

Healthcare and Medical Facilities

Tampa is well on its way to becoming increasingly well known for its world-class medical treatments and technology and state-of-the-art health care facilities.

The impact of our medical renaissance is such a vital component of Tampa's future that the Tampa Hillsborough Economic Development Corp. is positioning this area as a global leader in progressive health care.

That means living here will provide convenient access to some of the best places and practitioners for diagnosing, treating and curing serious injuries and life-threatening illnesses.

Highlights of Tampa's healthcare community include the following:

Moffitt Cancer Center is Florida's sole National Cancer Institute-designated comprehensive care center in Florida and among 41 nationwide. The designation acknowledges Moffitt's achievements in research, contributions to clinical trails, prevention and cancer control.

The main campus of Moffitt Cancer Center is located near the University of South Florida.

The $38 million, 90,000-square-foot University of South Florida's Center for Advanced Medical Learning and Simulation (CAMLS) located in downtown Tampa, is considered to be the largest facility of its kind. By combining high tech tools and simulation techniques, CAMLS provides state-of-the-art surgical training.

St. Joseph's Children's Hospital opened its Steinbrenner Children's Emergency/Trauma Center in late 2013 to better accommodate the demands of treating more than 45,000 children annually. The state-certified, level II pediatric trauma referral center is the busiest children's emergency center in the region.

This community also benefits from the major medical research conducted in area facilities. With the help of a healthy and well-established medical community, and its support industries, Tampa Bay residents receive top quality health care and medical services.

Hospitals and Health Care Providers

BayCare Health System, headquartered in Clearwater, is a community-wide, not-for-profit network of preventive, diagnostic and treatment centers and services that encompass non-profit hospitals, outpatient facilities and services ranging from imaging and labs to behavioral health and home health care. In 2014, BayCare welcomed a new Heart Institute at St. Joseph's Hospital. That 35,000-square-foot campus offers advanced, comprehensive cardiovascular care.

St. Joseph's Hospital, St. Joseph's Children's Hospital and St. Joseph's Women's Hospital are all part of the BayCare family and are located northwest of downtown Tampa, within close proximity of each other. St. Joseph's Hospital, with 870 beds, ranks as Tampa's second largest hospital. St. Joseph's Children's Hospital is recognized as the region's busiest children's emergency center. Other local BayCare Health System facilities include St. Joseph's Hospital - North in Lutz and South Florida Baptist Hospital, which offers full service care in Plant City.

Since opening in 1986, Moffitt Cancer Center has consistently been ranked among "America's Best Hospitals" for cancer care by *U.S. News & World Report* since 1999 while earning a worldwide reputation for quality care.

Contributing to the prevention and cure of cancer is the primary mission of this 206-bed, not-for-profit hospital. Its Cancer Center has one of the largest blood and bone marrow transplant programs in the Southeast, performing more than 400 transplants a year.

In addition to the main facility found near the University of South Florida campus, outpatient cancer care can also be accessed at a satellite location, the Moffitt Cancer Center at International Plaza. Construction of a new $74.2 million, 200,000-square-foot outpatient facility located less than a mile from the cancer center's main complex is expected to be completed by 2015.

Tampa General Hospital (TGH) is a private, not-for-profit 1,018-bed hospital located on Davis Islands. It is home to the region's only adult solid organ transplant center, Level 1 trauma center and burn unit. As one of Florida's largest hospitals, and among the region's largest employers, TGH has a distinguished history that includes the successful completion of the state's first heart transplant in 1985.

Tampa General Hospital consistently ranks among the leading hospitals in the country.

TGH is a state-certified comprehensive stroke center and its 32-bed, Neuroscience Intensive Care Unit is one of the largest on Florida's west coast. *U.S. News & World Report* named TGH the best hospital in this metropolitan area for 2013-14.

Established in 1927, TGH has served as the primary teaching hospital for the USF Health Morsani College of Medicine since the school's inception in the early 1970s and is the clinical site for associate, baccalaureate and graduate nursing programs for the University of South Florida, University of Tampa, Hillsborough Community College, St. Petersburg College and University of Florida.

James A. Haley Veterans' Hospital is a 415-bed hospital that also provides 118 beds at the nursing home care unit located on-site. A teaching hospital and a tertiary care facility, it is classified as a Clinical Referral Level 1 Facility. It was the first VA hospital to be designated as a Magnet Hospital, a national benchmark for excellence in nursing care.

The hospital consists of five Veterans Health Administration facilities (access points). Two are located in Tampa and New Port Richey, and three community-based outpatient clinics are found in Zephyrhills, Lakeland and Brooksville.

Shriners Hospital for Children Tampa specializes in caring for children requiring treatment for the following: orthopedic and neuromusculoskeletal conditions, burn and spinal cord injuries or cleft lip and palate procedures. This healthcare is provided without financial obligation to patients or families.

The Tampa location opened in 1985 and is one of 22 facilities of its kind in the U.S. Canada and Mexico.

Shopping

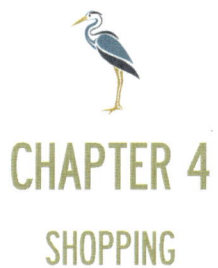

CHAPTER 4
SHOPPING

From Big Malls to Boutiques, Home Decor to Designer Fashions

Shopping opportunities throughout the Tampa Bay area range from major retail outlets to specialty stores, luxury to low-cost goods and brand new to gently used merchandise.

No single mall offers it all, but area wide there is a huge array of major department stores, chic boutiques, sources for everything from sportswear to formalwear and stores stocking hardware to hard-to-find products.

There was a time when names like Neiman Marcus, Tiffany and Louis Vuitton couldn't be found in Tampa. Thanks to a growing population, and the increasing disposable income of residents and visitors alike, we are now on a first name basis with Henri Bendel, Tory Burch and Michael Kors. But that doesn't mean we don't just as eagerly swarm H&M or check out the clearance racks at DSW Shoes or Nordstrom Rack.

Sure, we know our designers and long for those red carpet moments. But, we also love the outdoors where we can fish, swim, sail, hike, bike and hunt. One of the biggest outdoors stores in the country, Bass Pro Shops, has expanded to the Brandon area (east of Tampa) with a 140,000-square-foot destination store.

Major brand names and shops that are tops in their category are a big part of the local retail scene. Shop for the latest technology at the Apple Store or create a customized closet for shoes, clothes and accessories at The Container Store.

Tampa may not start many fashion trends but it certainly knows which ones to follow and how to work those looks. Each fall a collection of runway events and style seminars, known as Fashion Week, celebrate collections created by local designers. One of the Tampa's leading style-makers is the aptly named Judy Tampa whose designs are carried in stores throughout the country and in Canada. Locally, you can find her latest creations at South Tampa's Deborah Kent's.

Whatever the size of your budget, there are plenty of places to find top quality household goods from kitchen utensils at Williams-Sonoma to secondhand home decor from the fine furniture collections showcased at Britton Plaza's The Missing Piece.

Fill a room or complete a house with smart looking furnishings that won't bust your budget from IKEA. Outfit your kitchen with top-of-the-line culinary tools at the Rolling Pin Kitchen Emporium or create the stylish kitchen or bathroom of your dreams at the place with the most fashionable faucets and sleekest sinks, Ferguson's located in South Tampa's Willow Design District.

When you don't have the time to run all around town, you'll probably find that Hyde Park Village boasts the best range of merchandise to meet your needs. This open-air collection of shops and restaurants is quite walkable. On weekends, it hosts special events ranging from a monthly farmer's market to craft beer festivals. Many of its stores are found only in Tampa, but there are also familiar retail residents like Pottery Barn and Restoration Hardware.

For one of the most convenient retail collections where you can fill an eclectic shopping list, check out Walter's Crossing located at the intersection of North Dale Mabry Highway and I-275. Here you can browse for fashionable bargains at Nordstrom Rack, find stylish shoes at discount prices for the whole family at DSW, pick up your pet's favorite treats at PetSmart, re-stock the liquor cabinet at Total Wine & More, or get what is needed to build a liquor cabinet at Home Depot.

For haute couture and hot restaurants be sure to head for International Plaza. Here you can smartly outfit a home at the area's only Crate &

Shopping

Barrel Store or arm yourself with the latest Gucci handbag. The lively Bay Street area is an open-air section where locals love to flock for a post-shopping meal or show off their new outfits while dancing at Blue Martini.

Down the street, WestShore Plaza has more mainstream shopping opportunities, from Old Navy to Macy's and even Dick's Sporting Goods. Dining is a part of WestShore, too, including Seasons 52, P.F. Chang's and Mitchell's Fish Market, to name a few.

About 20 miles north of downtown Tampa off of I-75, Tampa Premium Outlets features brand names and well-known designers at discounted prices. Shop names such as Brooks Brothers, Disney, Gap, J Crew, Michael Kors, Nike, Saks Fifth Avenue, Steve Madden and Vera Bradley, without breaking the bank.

You need it, you name it, you can find it somewhere in Tampa Bay.

International Plaza offers a mix of fashionable boutiques, major department stores, specialty shops and places to dine.

Grocery & Gourmet Shopping

The Tampa area offers a wonderful selection of places to shop for food. Florida's nearly year-round growing season provides a variety of fresh-picked produce; the nearby Gulf of Mexico is brimming with plenty of fresh seafood. And, local farmers and ranchers are making it abundantly easier for both professional chefs and local residents to purchase locally sourced foods.

Filling a shopping list has never been so convenient and so rich with choices. From multi-national stores to mom-and-pop shops, you can find an increasingly diverse range of products ranging from imported items and familiar brand names to organically grown produce, fresh-from-the-oven, gluten-free baked goods and farm fresh eggs.

Supermarkets, weekly and monthly farmer's markets, produce stands, specialty stores, gourmet grocers and stores that feature a wide selection of "green," or more natural foods and products, round out the retail outlets available throughout the area.

At the top of the food store chain is Publix Supermarkets, which is headquartered in Lakeland, FL and founded in 1930. This is the largest and fastest-growing employee-owned supermarket in the U.S. It's almost impossible to drive more than a few blocks in any direction, without passing a Publix or a Publix GreenWise Market (South Tampa) that stocks all-natural and organic products. In addition to being prominent and dominant, the stores are known for outstanding family-friendly customer service.

Another grocery with deep ties to Florida is Winn-Dixie. The Jacksonville, Florida-based chain is a subsidiary of BI-LO Holdings, LLC, the 9th largest traditional supermarket chain in the nation, operating nearly 500 stores in Alabama, Florida, Georgia, Louisiana and Mississippi.

The Fresh Market began in North Carolina in 1982 but now has locations in 20 states, including two in Tampa, one in Clearwater and another in St. Petersburg. Whether buying ready-to-eat dishes or stocking up on basics, the choices are a bit more choice and the shelves are stocked with more out-of-the-ordinary brands and specialty items than more traditional groceries.

Whole Foods Market has two stores in Tampa and one in Clearwater. Known for natural and organic foods and products—from soaps to soups to pet food and fresh seafood—Whole Foods appeals to the health conscious carnivore as well as to the strict vegan or vegetarian. Try not to shop hungry—there are many made-to-order and ready-to-eat foods, including a salad bar and hot food bar And, lots of free samples throughout the store may be too tempting to pass up.

Another recent, and extremely economical, addition to the list of grocers is ALDI. Since opening its first Central Florida location in 2008, this discount grocer has already sprouted up quickly with three locations in Tampa, two in Brandon, one in Plant City and six in Pinellas County. ALDI carries a fraction of what competitors stock and the inventory is predominantly private label but cost savings can be significant.

In South Tampa, a family-owned and operated market offers raw honey, cage-free eggs, raw milk plus a variety of fresh vegetables. The South Tampa Farm lacks a big flashy sign and weekly ad fliers but it boasts farm-fresh foods from a farm founded more than 35 years ago.

If really going to the source is more your style, Sweetwater Organic Farm hosts a Sunday market from November to May that is very popular with families. The urban organic farm and environmental education center operates a Community Supported Agriculture (CSA) membership program that lets people pay to receive a weekly share of the harvest.

Independent businesses that specialize in gourmet and healthy foods include Duckweed Urban Market in downtown Tampa and The Corner Store in Plant City. A few years ago, Duckweed Urban Market relocated from its original downtown location into the lobby of a nearby high-rise residential tower making it easy for office workers and residents alike to buy craft beers, freshly squeezed juices, meats, sweets and many made-in-Tampa items like roasted coffee and honey. The Corner Store opened its doors in the historic downtown district of Plant City to provide seasonal produce and quality ingredients for home chefs. The owners, founders and creators of the concept incorporated locally sourced and re-purposed materials into the charming décor. They feature a made-from-scratch menu that offers a delicious selection of soups, salads and sandwiches. In addition to seasonings, sauces, produce and more sold at the store, it also stocks items crafted by local artists.

Eastern Hillsborough has lots of acreage dedicated to crops like strawberries and blueberries that invite the public out for dedicated u-pick times. But if you prefer picking up rather than picking, check out Parkesdale Farm Market, another Plant City fixture. It is said to be the largest strawberry and citrus market in the state. It's as popular for its fruits and vegetables as it is for the strawberry milkshakes, strawberry cookies and strawberry shortcake that is serves up on site.

Tampa's ethnic mix drives demand for specialty markets featuring a variety of cuisines. St. Petersburg's Mazzaro's Italian Market is considered a major destination for foodies and the ultimate shopping source for chefs. Under one sprawling roof is a wine and beer shop, cheese counter, butcher shop, bakery, freshly made pastas, coffee bar, fresh seafood section and more. Plan to spend a lot of time here to shop, eat and enjoy. Next-door is the large and lovely Casa di Mazzaro, which stocks cookware, housewares, teas and aprons to outdoor grilling utensils.

For something equally exotic, but a bit closer to home, explore the Oceanic Supermarket located on the outskirts of downtown Tampa. Tanks of live seafood, unfamiliar fresh produce, roasted duck and Oriental teas are just a sample of what awaits shoppers here. It is easy to feel as if you've been transported to Chinatown in San Francisco or New York while trying to decipher some of the store's signage and trying to determine just what those oddly shaped vegetables could possibly be or how they need to be prepared.

A favorite alternative to big box grocery stores are the various farmers' markets that set up weekly or monthly during much of the year. Typically, from fall through spring, vendors bring whatever is in season to designated areas for shoppers to select. The prices can be enticing, especially considering the quality and freshness of the produce. Many markets even offer fresh baked goods, private label hot sauces, artisan cheeses and much more. Bring a shopping bag, plenty of cash and arrive early for the best selection.

One of the most highly anticipated additions to the local retail mix is the arrival of California-based [Trader Joe's](#) making a grand entrance into this market with, not one, but two Tampa Bay locations, South Tampa and St. Petersburg. The popular shop is known for its eclectic mix of imported, private label and nicely priced foods and a good selection of well-priced wines, many which will be available here for the first time. Those in the know make sure to stock up during each visit to Trader Joe's because part of the adventure is its constantly changing inventory.

Major Shopping Malls

Tampa's Bay's large retail complexes range from enclosed to open-air and single-story to double-decker. All are filled with nationally known stores, chains and names as well as some only-in-Florida retailers. With movie complexes, sports bars and casual to fine dining options available at most malls, the opportunities to spend time—and money—while shopping, dining or being entertained are endless.

If one-stop shopping is your goal, check out the area's largest shopping complexes for the best variety of the latest fashions to leading beauty products, toys for girls and boys, athletic gear, keepsake jewelry to the latest, greatest electronics and cell phones.

[International Plaza and Bay Street](#)

This large, two-story shopping complex is complemented by Bay Street, an outdoor section lined with places to dine, drink and dance. This centrally located shopping destination is located near Tampa International Airport and Raymond James Stadium and connected to the Renaissance Tampa International Plaza Hotel.

[Tampa Premium Outlets](#)

More than 100 outlet shops await at Tampa Premium Outlets, about 20 miles north of downtown Tampa off of I-75. Top designers and brand names include Saks Fifth Avenue OFF 5TH, Polo Ralph Lauren Factory Store, NIKE Factory Store, Calvin Klein, Michael Kors, Coach Outlet, Tommy Hilfiger, Tumi, Under Armour and Cole Haan Outlet. The outdoor shopping mall is open seven days a week.

The Shoppes at Wiregrass

Wear—or be sure to buy—comfortable walking shoes when making your way through this open-air, 850-000-square-foot collection of retail and restaurant establishments. Its collection of anchor stores includes Dillard's, JCPenney and Macy's. If you work up an appetite walking around, there are nearly two dozen eateries offering frozen yogurt and wood-fired pizza to Philly steaks and sushi.

Westfield Brandon

The sprawling mall is bordered by multiple shopping centers making it one of the area's busiest places to park and among the most congested places to shop. But there's something to be said for having major department stores like Dillard's and Sears, leading discount stores like Target, and dozens of specialty stores so close together when you have a long list of gifts to buy.

Westfield Citrus Park

This mall seems to have it all. Think large-scale and long walks from end-to-end. It offers shoppers five anchor stores, a multi-plex movie theater, several restaurants, a food court and even Atomic Tattoos for piercings and body art.

Westshore Plaza

The area's first fully enclosed and air-conditioned shopping center, WestShore remains a popular shopping spot and place to see first-run movies at the AMC multi-plex. The food court is a great place for a quick bite or a healthy snack. For full service dining, select from Sansei Japan, Mitchell's Fish Market, Maggiano's Little Italy, and P.F. Chang's

Hyde Park Village

This picturesque, open-air collection of stores, restaurants and a movie theater is nestled in the neighborhood of Hyde Park. Restaurants and shops blend locally-owned, independent businesses with well known national and regional chains.

Shopping for Bargains and Good Causes

Consignment, second hand and thrift shops offer an ever-changing selection of clothes, coats, purses, accessories, home decor and more throughout the year.

LifePath Hospice Thrift Stores

Sales of gently used to brand new clothes, furniture, books and other items support LifePath Hospice patient and family programs.

The Spring Boutique

Sales of donated clothing, furniture and household goods from two locations provide shelter and support for victims of domestic abuse.

Goodwill Industries - Suncoast Inc.

Sales of new and used clothes, furniture, household items and more support employment services and training programs for people with barriers to employment.

Salvation Army

Sales of furniture, clothing, household goods and more fund adult rehabilitation centers that offer housing, work, group and individual therapy.

Consignment, Secondhand, Name Brand

Mosh Post Designer Consignment Boutique

High-end purses, shoes and apparel guaranteed to be authentic.

Plato's Closet

Gently worn top-name brands and on-trend clothes for men and women.

The Missing Piece

Consignment shop features furnishings for every room and any lifestyle.

Triage Consignment Showcase

Family owned and operated consignment shop specializes in upscale women's clothing and home furnishings.

Play It Again Sports

Multiple locations throughout the Tampa area specialize in new and used sports and fitness equipment.

Shopping for clothes at Triage Consignment Showcase

Vintage, Classic and Retro Clothing & Household Goods

Boots, wigs, clothes, furniture and more can be found at Squaresville.

La France

This Ybor City store offers a stylish array of men's and women's fashions from throughout the ages, think Gatsby to the go go days of disco.

Sherry's YesterDAZE Vintage Clothing & Antiques

Located in Seminole Heights, this is where to go for fun to funky furniture, fine to costume jewelry and clothes from the late 1800s to early 1990s for men and women.

Squaresville Vintage & New Clothing, Retro Home Decor

To-die-for tie dye shirts, Elvis memorabilia, wild wigs and all things rock 'n roll plus furnishings for that 1950s feel and flair.

New to Re-Purposed, Recycled and Salvaged Furnishings, Lighting Fixtures & More

Blue Moon Trading Co.

One-of-a-kind pieces will highlight any room in your home. You'll find new merchandise from top names as well as pieces that have been re-purposed or custom built.

Magnolia Inspiring Interiors

Located in a restored 1923 grocery and pharmacy, discover everything from delicate jewelry to fine furnishings and original art to seasonal decorations that add fun and flair to any interior.

MarketPlace Interiors

Antique, vintage and new furniture are creatively showcased using vignettes created by various interior designers. There's the 4,000-square-foot indoor space plus an outdoor area for fountains, statues and benches. Located in the Willow Design District.
www.addisondicus.com/info/design-center

Custom pieces to re-purposed items from Blue Mooncreate one-of-a-kind interior designs.

Shopping

Schiller's Architectural and Design Salvage

Source for replacement home design or reclaimed home decor elements that can be used to construct a work-in-progress or create a new look with vintage elements.

Books, Magazines, Music and More

Barnes & Noble

Bestsellers, broad range of topics and current newspapers and magazines are part of the expansive inventory featured here. Curl up in a chair and sip something from the in-store café while you browse. Two stores: 213 N. Dale Mabry and 11802 N. Dale Mabry

Inkwood Books

This local independent bookstore stocks new books, regularly hosts author events and can accommodate readers of all ages and all interests. It is located in a former house in the South Howard (SoHo) area of the city.

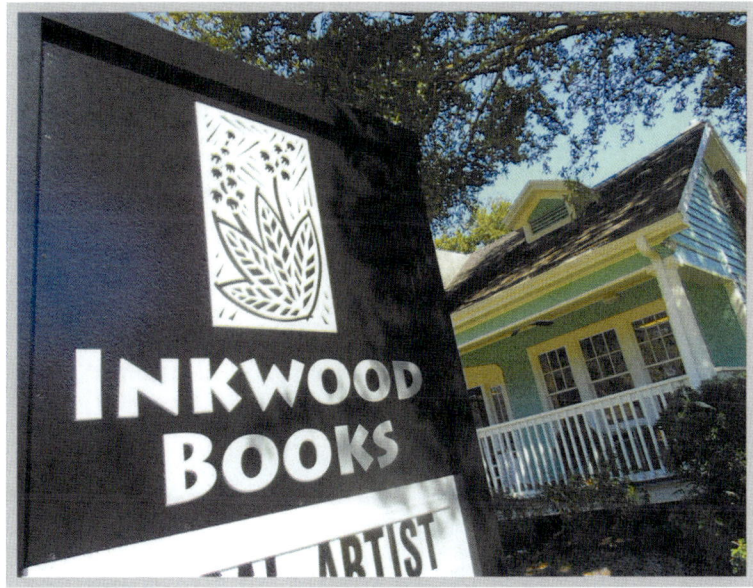

Inkwood Books is an independent bookstore located in Tampa's SoHo neighborhood.

Old Tampa Book Company

Like its name implies, this is the place to hunt for used, rare and out-of-print books with many nicely priced. This street-front shop is centrally located in downtown Tampa.

The Bookstore at the Oxford Exchange

This curated collection of classic to contemporary books covers a wide spectrum of subjects that include fiction, travel, history, science, medicine and business.

Oxford Exchange near downtown Tampa offers a bookstore, a retail area with home decor to fashionable jewelry, a restaurant and both a coffee and tea counter.

Haslam's Book Store

Located in St. Petersburg, this is Florida's largest new and used bookstore. John and Mary Haslam first opened it in 1933 and the business continues to be operated by a third generation of family members.

Microgroove

Vinyl reigns supreme at Microgroove in Tampa's Seminole Heights neighborhood. The independent record store buys and sells new and used vinyl records of all genres, with a few CDs mixed in for good measure.

Banana's

This long-standing St. Petersburg source for music, movies and more fills 17,000 square feet—spread over two stores—with its vast musical collection. *Rolling Stone Magazine* ranks it among the top record stores in the country.

Mojo Books & Music

A rare independent used book and record store, it also operates a coffee and tea bar on-site along with offering a selection of posters, T-shirts and other memorabilia.

Sound Exchange

Three Tampa Bay locations feature new and used CDs, DVDs, video games, vinyl records, books and select stereo equipment.

More Shopping Trip Tips

Museums, attractions and non-profits throughout the Tampa Bay area generally feature gift shops stocked with books, jewelry, apparel, crafts and other items that can't be found at more traditional stores. Consider the Tampa Bay History Museum, Henry B. Plant Museum, Big Cat Rescue, Tampa Museum of Art, Florida Aquarium and other similar non-profits when looking for a special gift.

Farmer's markets are most often associated with food but can also be great sources for handmade items ranging from woven baskets to wood crafts and scented soaps to original paintings. Likewise, that's also true for annual festivals, arts shows and other special events.

Costco, Sam's Club and BJ's Wholesale Club are membership warehouses in the Tampa Bay area offering electronics to pet food, automotive supplies to cosmetics. But their big claim to fame would be the ability to buy in bulk.

Weekend garage sales and flea markets can be fun for those who enjoy the art of the hunt. Flea markets tend to operate throughout the year and through all kinds of weather. When someone invites you "saling" for the weekend they don't mean boating. They mean hitting neighborhoods to check for signs announcing "Multi-Household Yard Sale." Check online or local newspapers for listings for Friday, Saturday and Sunday yard sales and go early to get the best selection. If one-strop shopping is more your thing, the Big Top Flea Market in North Tampa is said to be the biggest and best of its kind, occupying more than 36 acres accommodating hundreds of vendors.

Filling You in on Fashion Finds

The Tampa Bay region is filled with shopping, retail and a love for fashion, from destination malls like International Plaza and Bay Street to trendy boutique shopping in Hyde Park Village and Sundial St. Pete. People visit the region from abroad to shop designer garments and vintage treasures.

HSN corporate headquarters is located in St. Petersburg and their campus hosts leading national and international fashion, accessory and beauty products and personalities, including: Liz Lange, Rhonda Shear, Iman, Diane Gilman, Vince Camuto and more. In addition, HSN brings celebrity power to the region through its collaborations with everyone from Jessica Simpson to Serena Williams. Overall, the region

Nancy Vaughn

boasts more than 30+ malls and shopping centers, with recent additions like: The Mall at University Town Center, Tampa Premium Outlets, and The Shops at Wiregrass.

Such esteemed information outlets as the *New York Times* salute Tampa for its hidden shopping gems, encouraging local shoppers to feed their vintage cravings at a variety of consignment shops including: La France in Ybor City, MISRED Outfitters in downtown St. Petersburg, Sherry's YesterDaze Vintage in Seminole Heights, and Revolve Clothing Exchange with location in South Tampa, St. Pete and Ybor. You can buy, sell or trade at many of these shops and find garments from decades ago or gently used labels of today. If you're looking for luxury clothing at a discount, you can try J'adore Designer Boutique in Carrollwood, Mosh Posh, and Repeat Performance Boutique in South Tampa. For shoppers who don't want to commit, the latest styles and leading designers are available in abundance at Lending Luxury. There you can rent your next lavish outfit.

Fashion designers from various parts of the U.S. participate in the region's official Tampa Bay Fashion Week held annually each Fall. The event is marked by a series of runway shows, boutique vendor pop-ups, fashion seminars, styling sessions and parties. This event brings talented fashion and accessories designers to Tampa Bay to showcase their work for local, regional and national retail buyers and boutique owners as well as style-conscious consumers.

In addition, local business partners, aspiring models and community members have an opportunity to get a firsthand look at styles displayed by these fashion trendsetters and become inspired by the creativity and positive, high-fashion and artistic energy, that make this week a major event.

There definitely is an emerging local fashion scene that highlights the region's homegrown fashion and accessories design talent.

Tampa Bay-based fashion designers include the following: Rhonda Shear of Rhonda Shear Intimates, Elizabeth Carson Racker Designs, Floridita Swimwear, Sandra Hagen, and more.

The various designers specialize in a range of garments from couture to ready-to-wear.

Shoppers can have their own, custom-made garment created by fashion design talents who reside in our region. Imagine walking away with a one-of-a-kind creation.

In addition, various other fashion industry players, including hair/make-up artists, fashion stylists, photographers and more, also reside in the region and contribute to the growing interest and influence of Tampa Bay fashion. Lifestyle publications including: *Bay Magazine, Tampa Bay METRO,* and T*ampa Bay Style* regularly feature the best in local fashion, along with *Tampa Bay Times' Deal Divas*, who share the area's affordable fashion and shopping finds. There is also a post-education school, The Art Institute of Tampa, that educates future trendsetters in the industry.

If you're looking for some style and great shopping in Florida, Tampa Bay should be on your list. It's a Florida must-have and a great accessory to the fashion industry and shopping scene!

NANCY VAUGHN
White Book Agency
www.whitebookagency.com

CHAPTER 5
THINGS TO DO

Tampa loves to have fun, get outdoors, throw parties and just generally celebrate what's great about this area.

This is a place where people love to make the most of being outdoors. With water, water everywhere, many more sunny than grey days and lots of trails to run, ride, rollerblade and hike, Tampa offers a multitude of ways to seek entertainment, exercise and enjoyment.

There's sure to be something happening year round but most major annual events occur from fall through spring to avoid the heat, rain, humidity and possibility of storms that can hamper attendance during summer.

Even native Floridians have their limits when it comes to weathering the weather. Still, hardly a weekend arrives without heralding some arts event, a new theatrical performance or annual celebration, like the Florida State Fair, concert in the park or some other crowd-pleasing activity.

Moving to Tampa

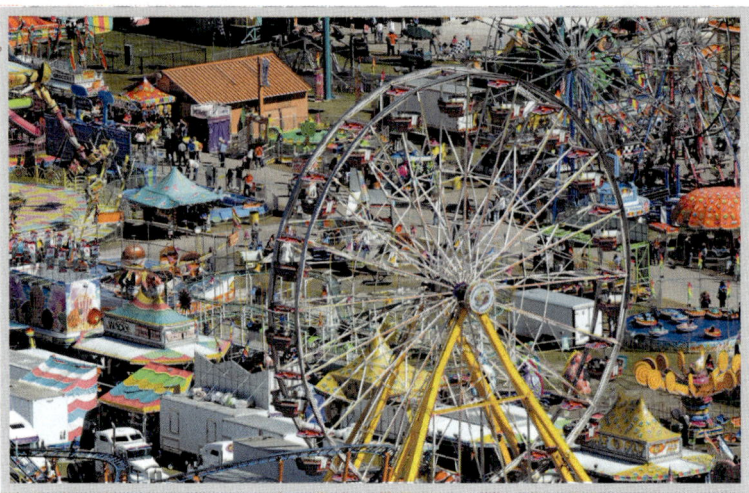

The Florida State Fair is one of Tampa's most popular winter events

Both the weather and wealth of natural beauty make it irresistible to get outdoors for much of the year, whether to enjoy a picnic, paddle a canoe or kayak along the waterfront, participate in group rides with the area's popular bike peddling groups or compete for real, or for real fun, while running any of the many local race events.

Not quite so inclined to be quite so active? Cheer from the stands at a professional sports event, call for an encore at an opera or classical music concert, play a round at local golf courses, call the shots at tennis courts or set sail for a sunset cruise. And, that's just a few of the ways we like to play.

The mix of things to do, places to go and special events to see, and be seen is expansive but not necessarily expensive. Many activities are free, require only a modest admission price or offer advance ticket purchase discounts.

Things to Do

Golfers enjoy year-round access to the links throughout the Tampa area

Festivals

Festival season begins in January in Tampa and runs through the spring, taking a hiatus during the summer months and resuming in the fall, and there's pretty much something for everyone!

Perhaps most popular of all the festivals is Gasparilla, which even has its own season. Named after pirate Jose Gaspar, the city of Tampa turns pirate in January with the Children's Gasparilla Extravaganza and the adult-geared Gasparilla Pirate Fest, both of which feature miles-long parades down Bayshore Boulevard, complete with pirates and bead throwing.

Gasparilla season continues into March with the Gasparilla Festival of the Arts, Gasparilla International Film Festival and the Gasparilla Music Festival. Though they all share the same name, each is independently operated, but all are loads of fun. Also in March, Tampa Pride takes place, and in April Tampa goes Italian with Festa Italiana.

Events start to wind down for the summer as temperatures rise, and pick back up again in October with the Tampa International Gay

& Lesbian Film Festival and Halloween-themed Guavaween in Ybor City, and then the Outback Bowl festivities in December.

Sporting Life

There's no shortage of professional sports here or any sorts of sports, for that matter. The region is home to the NFL's Tampa Bay Buccaneers football team, NHL's Tampa Bay Lightning hockey team, MLB's Tampa Bay Rays baseball team, NASL's Tampa Bay Rowdies soccer team and Arena Football's Tampa Bay Storm.

Major League Baseball spring training camps held locally include the New York Yankees at Tampa's Steinbrenner Field, the Philadelphia Phillies in Clearwater and the Toronto Blue Jays in Dunedin.

Collegiate sports schedules are offered by both the University of South Florida (USF) and the University of Tampa (UT).

Two post-season college football bowl games call Tampa Bay home. The former Beef 'O' Brady's Bowl/St. Petersburg Bowl is held late December at Tropicana Field in downtown St. Petersburg and features a bowl-eligible team from the Big East Conference competing with one from Conference USA.

The Outback Bowl is played in Raymond James Stadium on New Year's Day and pits teams from the SEC and Big Ten Conference. Ray Jay, as it is commonly referred to, is also the home field for the Buccaneers and the NCAA USF Bulls. Ray Jay has hosted two Super Bowls, in 2001 and 2009. But the first two Super Bowls held in Tampa were in 1984 and 1991 and were played at Ray Jay's predecessor, the former Tampa Stadium/Houlihan's Stadium/Big Sombrero.

In addition, we serve up a year-round calendar of amateur, youth and premier sports competitions. Ranging from Dragon Boat racing events to NCAA Final Four basketball games, these special events bring athletes from around the world to the area.

For information about upcoming athletic events, the Tampa Bay Sports Commission provides news about everything from international wakeboard competitions to NCAA championships being held in the Tampa Bay area.

Heart for the Arts

Our lively local performing and visual arts scene includes galleries, museums, opera companies, touring productions of Broadway hits, local theatrical groups and indoor and outdoor concert venues attracting major musical groups, solo artists and rock bands to top DJs who do their thing at Raymond James Stadium, the Amelia Arena, where the NHL Lightning compete, MIDFLORIDA Credit Union Amphitheatre and the USF Sun Dome, to name a few venues.

One of the most popular ways to see a diverse group of musical acts is during the annual Florida Strawberry Festival in Plant City. An open-air stadium hosts top talent for ticket prices that can range from free to double digits. The yearly celebration of Plant City's world famous strawberry crop has been country strong for years but now offers a blend of performers appealing to a wider range of musical tastes and ages. Mixed in with Little Big Town, The Band Perry and Oak Ridge Boys are groups like Styx and performers like Brenda Lee.

Plant City produces the world's leading strawberry crop each winter

For a fun way to enjoy that next big blockbuster, independent or foreign film, head for the historic, beautifully ornate, Tampa Theatre in downtown Tampa. The Baroque-style film house was proclaimed "one of the world's most beautiful theaters" by the BBC in 2013. Best known for showing classic to contemporary movies, live entertainment occasionally fills the bill there as well. Among past performers are Arlo Guthrie, David Byrne and Colbie Caillat, Jimmy Fallon and Andrew Dice Clay. The 1926 movie theatre offers backstage-to-balcony tours and music performed live on its Mighty Wurlitzer just before the start of most movies.

The Tampa Theatre ranks among the most beautiful theaters in the world

The David A. Straz Center for the Performing Arts boasts one of the biggest and most diverse entertainment arrays in Florida with its straight-from-Broadway touring productions of Tony-award winning plays and musicals, Florida Orchestra concerts, elaborate productions of top operas, world-class classical musicians, Grammy-award winning artists, ballet troupes, modern dance companies and much more that populate any—or all—of its five theaters on almost a nightly basis. Theaters range from an intimate 130-seat venue to the 2,610-seat Carol Morsani Hall.

Downtown has evolved into a cultural hub for the Tampa arts scene because of its collection of museums, historic sites and theatrical facilities.

Just across the Hillsborough River is the University of Tampa where the Henry B. Plant Museum is housed. The Plant Museum preserves the original look and lifestyle that made the former Tampa Bay Hotel a high-end, winter resort when it opened in 1891. In addition to recreating the decor of the guest rooms, the museum hosts special exhibits typically tied to Tampa's past.

The Straz Performing Arts Center brings dazzling entertainment to downtown Tampa year round

Closer to the downtown core is an outstanding collection of arts and entertainment facilities that include intriguing exhibits featured at the Florida Museum of Photographic Arts. The Tampa Museum of Art is a stunning structure with an even more impressive ability to attract exceptional artworks to its galleries. Completing that cultural scene is the playful Glazer Children's Museum and the interactive and informative Tampa Bay History Museum.

Tampa's got talent. The professional artists who live and work locally are living proof, occasionally opening up their studios for special tours or fundraising events best illustrate that. Susan Gott is one local resident and award-winning glass artist whose work has been commissioned and collected worldwide. Bleu Acier is a studio owned by a talented couple who are both renowned artists in their own right: Erika Greenberg-Schneider and Dominique Labauvie.

She is a master printmaker and he is an accomplished sculptor and painter. Their live/work space is also a venue for showcasing works by other esteemed artists.

The Gasparilla Festival of the Arts is not only Tampa's best known and best-attended arts-related event but it is one of the highest-rated outdoor shows of its kind in the country. This is a juried show offering serious prize money for fine art and fine crafts.

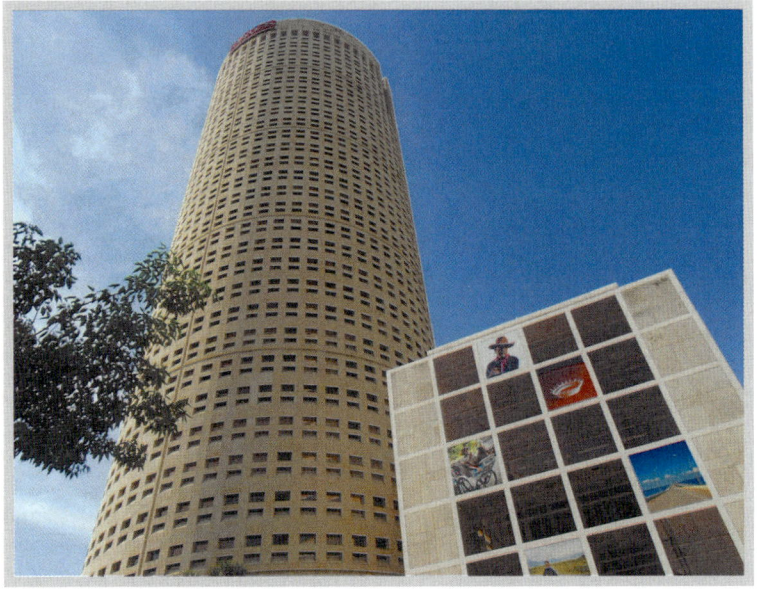

Florida Museum of Photographic Arts in downtown Tampa

Many fine galleries represent local to international artists. When it comes to special exhibits, Gallery 221 at the Hillsborough Community College Campus in Tampa, is greatly admired for curating really creative art events that have built quite a following, generating crowds at its opening events. The exceptional exhibits range from folk art to three-dimensional pieces throughout the year, frequently showcasing artists with ties to the local area.

The Arts Council of Hillsborough County is an excellent resource for information about upcoming events, venues, classes and workshops related to the arts.

Things to Do

Culinary Arts

Tampa is becoming increasingly known as a food scene that features a mix of landmark restaurants, farm-to-fork dining spots, movable feasts served up by food trucks and newcomers to the dining scene as well as new concepts that grew into global brands.

Food trucks from throughout Florida and as far away as Canada helped set a world record in 2013

Want to catch the next celebrity chef? The Culinary Arts and Design School at the Art Institute of Tampa operates "The Tutored Chef" restaurant that is open to the public for lunch and dinner when classes are in session. Watch chefs at work in the kitchen through the clear glass windows that let guests observe while they dine on delightfully delicious dishes created before their eyes. A big plus is that prices are well below what comparable fare would fetch at comparable restaurants.

A philosophy of *"if you can make it here you can make it anywhere,"* continues as other newcomers extend their own brand of hospitality statewide and out-of-state. The Tampa Bay area has proved to be a proving ground for new restaurant concepts. Outback Steakhouse restaurants, part of the Bloomin' Brands family, got its start here and the history of Hooters can be traced to its first location in Clearwater.

Restaurants boasting the deepest roots in Tampa's culinary development are the acclaimed Bern's Steak House and Columbia Restaurant.

Bern's, is one of a kind, world-famous for its aged steaks, comprehensive wine collection and decadent array of some 50 desserts as well as more than 1,000 dessert wines and spirits served in the Harry Waugh Dessert Room. It has been a favorite of world leaders, celebrities and the rich and famous for decades as well as a popular spot for locals since 1956. Bern's is best known for its steaks but offers a wide selection of dishes, including 21 types of caviar. Wine cellar and kitchen tours are available to all guests and both offer impressive behind-the-scenes looks at this legendary operation.

A more contemporary, seasonal style of cuisine is served at SideBern's a separate but related dining venture that is located on the same street as Bern's. Since joining SideBern's in 2008, Chef Chad Johnson has been honored as a James Beard semi-finalist for Best Chef. He continues to flex his culinary muscles while dividing his time at the latest addition to the Laxer family empire, Elevage at The Epicurean Hotel. The Epicurean is a 137-room boutique-style hotel that includes its signature restaurant, a patisserie, 40-seat culinary theater, spa, wine store and rooftop bar. Opened in late 2013, the hotel is directly across the street from Bern's.

[Bern's and the new Epicurean Hotel are both located in Tampa's SoHo district]

The original Columbia Restaurant, located in Ybor City, is a two-story, beautifully ornate landmark building spanning an entire city block. Founded in 1905 by Cuban immigrant Casimiro Hernandez Sr., it is the oldest restaurant in Florida and the largest Spanish restaurant in the world.

The Columbia now has seven distinctive locations in Florida including a cafe at Tampa International Airport. It has been owned and operated by the same family for five generations and remains a favorite destination dining spot for families, couples and groups to enjoy, not only outstanding food and a celebrated selection of more than 1,000 wines presented on a 240-plus page wine list, but also great entertainment. Flamenco/Spanish classical dance performances are available exclusively at the Ybor City restaurant nightly, except Sundays.

Flamenco dancers perform at the Columbia Restaurant in Ybor City

Not content to rest on this landmark restaurant's laurels, one of the patriarchs of the Columbia Restaurant, Richard Gonzmart, has created a new concept opening in an historic building located on the outskirts of downtown Tampa in 2014. Ulele honors the original Native American Indian inhabitants of this area by fusing elements from their culture with other cultural influences and utilizing indigenous ingredients from local waters and farms to create a new, different and dynamic dining experience.

Another of Richard Gonzmart's ideas has come to life with the re-opening of Tampa institution Goody Goody in Hyde Park. Originally opened in 1925, Gonzmart and his team reimagined the hamburger restaurant, using original recipes for its breakfast, lunch and dinner menus. Be sure to try the butterscotch pie—it's a locals' favorite.

The Tampa area has not always been noted for haute cuisine but that is changing as restaurants and chefs gain professional recognition, garnering James Beard nominations and attracting Food Network TV crews shooting on-location segments at local favorites like Taco Bus, which grew from a single food truck to multiple bus-themed dining spots featuring authentic Mexican food. Other nationally televised segments featured [Skipper's Smokehouse](), known for its, rustic setting and Florida seafood. Its popular Skipperdome features live music from all genres and performers from all over the globe.. Another featured food spot is [Tampa Bay Brewing Company](), a family-owned on-site microbrewery and restaurant that incorporates many of its craft beers into the dishes it serves.

The on-going popularity of food trucks reached a milestone in 2013. The Florida State Fairgrounds in Tampa hosted a one-day event billed as the "World's Largest Food Truck Rally" that attracted mobile chefs from around the state and across the country to Tampa to set a new record of 99 trucks.

Craft beer and brewpubs continue to come on strong locally as new breweries, tasting rooms and beer-inspired dining spots cater to micro-brew fans—there are more than 60 craft breweries in the Tampa Bay area. [Cigar City Brewing]() continues to reign as the area's leader for its award-winning brews. Its growing brand now includes a brewpub as well as the first airport brewpub in the country at Tampa International Airport.

Craft distilleries are now starting to crop up around the area as small batch production facilities of premium to flavored spirits gain in popularity. Some feature Florida-grown ingredients and others specialize in signature lines of rums, vodkas, whiskeys and more. [Twisted Sun Rum]() is one of the new brands and will likely launch the first Tampa-based production facility with a projected opening in 2016.

Things to Do

Cigar City Brewpub combines Cuban, Southern and Italian cuisine with Cigar City Brewery craft beers

Wonderful Dining Choices: Tampa Offers Many Ways to Dial Up the Culinary Fun

Tampa offers many ways to dial up the culinary fun.

Before selecting a choice on a menu, there is the daunting task of picking from a galaxy of creative dining options.

Hyde Park Village's On Swann shines, displaying the creative genius of Chef Chris Ponte (find him also at Café Ponte in Clearwater). Enjoy short ribs with citrus, pine nut crumbs, scallops with Brussels sprouts, and cobia with jasmine risotto and orange saffron nage. The white jacket maestro recommends a serving board of artisan-cured meats, cheeses, pate and mousse to share.

Mary Scourtes

Grey Salt, in the Seminole Hard Rock Hotel & Casino Tampa, is an elevated, Mediterranean and Italian-inspired oasis, a respite from the hustle of the nearby gaming tables. Enjoy duck breast, bouillabaisse and flatbreads with signature cocktails. A bonus is visiting with owner/celebrity chef Marc Murphy of television "Chopped" fame when he is in town.

Seminole Heights feeds its neighborhood in style. Culinary Institute of America-trained, Noel Cruz returned home from New York to open immensely popular Ichicoro Ramen. Ichicoro, which translates as "getting it right the first time," offers an array of aromatic dishes to ramen devotees. With true passion and proper techniques, Ferrell Alvarez, Rooster & The Till's co-owner/chef, handcrafts a memorable, farm-to-table experience.

Despite worry warts who tell us to eschew red meat, we return to one of Tampa's most famous landmarks, Bern's Steak House. An internationally known, encyclopedia-of-the-vine wine list offers unexpected, by-the-glass wines, fresh muddled juices and inventive combinations. Bern's aged, art of steaks, precisely defined by weight, thickness and requested temperature, come out impressively tender.

Oystercatcher's is essentially a vehicle for immaculate fish and a beautiful view, while sister restaurant, Armani's, with scenic views of Old Tampa Bay from its 14th-floor dining rooms, charms with inventive Italian cuisine.

Tampa's oldest restaurant, Ybor City's Columbia, is run by multiple generations of the Gonzmart dynasty. Brothers CEO/President Richard and Chairman of the Board Casey, maintain their family's culinary heritage at their 111-year-old restaurant. Flamenco shows add to the fun as one enjoys the substantial 1905 salad that can suffice as a meal.

Richard's Ulele ("You-lay-lee") honors a legendary princess at his distinctive, repurposed water works building overlooking the Hillsborough River. The menu fuses Native-American and multicultural influences with Florida's best water and land ingredients (try grilled oysters, pork shank, crab/mac and cheese, and homemade ice cream.) Handcrafted beer is brewed on the premises.

Chef Marty Blitz of Mise en Place (say Meez) has been serving distinctive nouveau American cuisine for about 30 years. He has been recognized on the local and national stage for good reason. The place's upscale feel, vibrant charm and changing menu keeps locals returning. Blitz and co-owner Maryann Ferenc are well respected for their commitment to the community.

Kevin and Karyn Kruszewski of Pane Rustica have the right motto: serve food so good you can taste the emotion baked in. They bake thousands of loaves of European breads and other baked specials each week.

Jeannie Pierola of Edison: Food + Drink Lab creates layer-on-layer flavors such as Madras-Seared Red Snapper with kumquat kimchee and Sesame Chile Yellowfin Tuna Burger with eggplant caponata, and espelette aioli.

Early bricklayers flattened "mixto" sandwiches between bricks to sear flavors of Cuban sandwiches made with Genoa salami, baked ham, pork, and Swiss cheese on crusty bread. Wright's Gourmet House's Cuban sandwiches are the gold standard, taking first place, almost forever, in the contests held by *The Tampa Tribune*. I had the pleasure of being part of the judging for many years.

Souvlaki, Moussaka, Pastitsio, and baklava are part of the good Greek takeaways from Louis Pappas' Market Cafes.

Who doesn't crave Pad Thai, with pork, chicken or tofu and peanuts, bean sprouts, and scallions? It reigns at south Tampa staples: Royal Palace Thai Restaurant, Thai Island, and Jasmine Thai.

 An unusual trip to the Wat Mongkolratanaram (about a half-mile from U.S. 41 on the banks of the Palm River) is a mind-blowing cook-a-thon each Sunday.

> Chinese, Indian, Vietnamese, Lebanese, Japanese, Ethiopian and other local restaurants help make Tampa a micro United Nations of cuisines.
>
> Tampa's high-end steak playground also includes national chains: Capitol Grill, Eddie V's, Flemings Prime Steakhouse and Ruth's Chris Steak House. The Outback Steak House brand started in Tampa.
>
> Welcome to Tampa; have fun exploring your own favorites.
>
> **Mary D. Scourtes**
>
> Former newspaper food critic and food editor and currently a freelance writer for local and national publications.

Spectacular Points of View

Enjoy a sunrise or sunset run along Bayshore Boulevard, the world's longest, continuous sidewalk that winds along the waterfront for more than four miles. It's quite a sight to watch the tides of people go by night and day while walking dogs, pushing strollers, riding bikes, roller blading or leisurely strolling. And, it's a wonderful vantage point for watching birds diving into the water and dolphins swimming by.

The Tampa Riverwalk is a paved, pedestrian friendly stretch that winds along and around downtown's waterfront. This urban pathway borders the business district and runs from the Channel District past the Tampa Bay History Center and Tampa Bay Forum and along the channel that leads to the Tampa Convention Center. From there it continues to Curtis Hixon Waterfront Park that borders the Tampa Museum of Art, Glazer Children's Museum and Florida Photography Museum before continuing on to the Straz Performing Arts Center.

One of the newest dedicated scenic stretches for walkers and bikers is a paved path that parallels the Courtney Campbell Causeway connecting Tampa with Clearwater and Safety Harbor. The Courtney Campbell Trail is a scenic stretch spanning Tampa Bay that is off limits to cars and fishing and represents the first phase of a project that will eventually extend to connect trails in both Hillsborough and

Pinellas counties. The four-mile-long, 16-foot-wide trail rises 45 feet above the water to provides breathtaking views.

Perks of Parks

One of the many perks of living here is the abundance of city and county parks. Curtis Hixon Waterfront Park in downtown Tampa is one of the area's most popular venues for musical groups, food festivals, seasonal activities, like the ice skating rinks that pops up during the holidays, and special events.

Plenty of public parks and playgrounds are open year round. Whether you want to reserve a site for a family picnic, watch your children play in the water-themed splash pad or swim in the pool or take a scenic hike, free city parks provide endless fun and good exercise.

County parks generally require a modest admission fee particularly if plans include launching a boat or camping overnight. Youth sports leagues and special camps and programs are also available but may require fees and registration.

View from Picnic Island Park located in Port Tampa

Area Attractions

While people travel from around the globe to enjoy these only-in-Tampa attractions, they are available year round for those who live here.

Busch Gardens began as a brewery and a garden spot filled with exotic birds. Birds are still part of the theme park's "residents" but beer is no longer being brewed there. Instead major thrill rides, state-of-the-art roller coasters, all sorts of exotic animals, live entertainment and a children's area designed with a Sesame Street theme, make this family-friendly attraction popular for all ages. The 297-acre park is considered one of the country's premier zoos with more than 12,000 animals. It also caters the thrill-ride enthusiasts who enjoy dropping from significant heights while traveling and exhilarating speeds.

Nearby Busch is the largest science center in the Southeast, the Museum of Science and Industry which has more than 450 hands-on exhibits incorporating scientific principals in fun, fascinating ways. Kids in Charge! is a designated area for youngsters, 12 and under, that has age-appropriate activities within a bright, light filled building. Recent additions to MOSI include the popular Sky Trail Ropes Course that invites adventurous types to test their skills of balance—and their ability to remain calm—while they climb and cross ropes, blocks and narrow tracks well above ground or go for the fast track and use the zip line to return to ground level.

Lowry Park Zoo earns high marks for family fun and provides fascinating looks at all types of animals in specially designed exhibits that eschew cages. More than 1,000 animals from around the world, as well as throughout Florida, are housed in natural habitats found within the nearly 60-acre site. The zoo is also home to a hospital for injured or ill manatees rescued from the wild, brought there to be treated and healed, before being returned to their natural habitat. Visitors can actually watch these enchanting, endangered creatures from a below water level viewing area that puts people face-to-face with manatees.

Things to Do

Lowry Park Zoo features a below-water viewing area that provides a perfect place to watch manatees in their natural habitat

Another free site to check out manatees is the Manatee Viewing Center, perched along the edge of Tampa Bay in Apollo Beach. Visit the open-air decks that lookout over the water during cold weather. The saltwater that originates in Tampa Bay is warmed as it flows through the Big Bend Power Station TECO facility. When the clean water is discharged back into the bay, the temperature provides critical protection from cold water for manatees, drawing them close to the shore for easy viewing.

Within viewing distance of the downtown Tampa Skyline and the Port Tampa Bay cruise ship terminals is the splashy Florida Aquarium, that features an outdoor water fun zone for youngsters and fascinating ways to view underwater worlds occupied byotters to alligators and from stingrays to moray eels, all within the 250,000-square-foot facility.

Rounding out the activities roster offered around the area is the Seminole Hard Rock Hotel & Casino, which ranks among the world's largest gambling and gaming establishments, and Tampa Bay Downs, a thoroughbred race track that has been a Tampa institution for nearly 90 years.

Moving to Tampa

The Seminole Hard Rock Hotel & Casino offers fine dining, musical entertainment and ranks among the largest gambling and gaming establishments worldwide

CHAPTER 6

FROM PRE-K TO POST GRAD: CHILDCARE AND EDUCATION

Tampa has a lot to offer families. Deciding where to live, what schools to attend and whether any sort of day care is needed are critical factors that families must consider when determining whether to make Tampa their new home.

Infant and Toddler Care

Based on nationwide averages of childcare rates, DayCareMatch.com ranks Tampa among the least expensive cities for costs associated with a toddler attending a site-based care facility for five days a week. In 2013, the average weekly rate in Tampa totaled $241 for the care of a single child, according to the site.

Of course, that rate can vary according to the level of childcare service provided. Types of service may cost more or less depending on whether the caregiver is to look after an infant or if older children require after school care. Whether supervision is needed for a half- to full-day as well as what, if any, additional services may be needed, like meals and transportation, will also factor into the equation. With so many variables to consider, it can be confusing and time-consuming to make realistic comparisons. Fortunately, there are free resources that may make what can be an overwhelming process much more manageable.

The Florida Department of Children and Families oversees statewide licensing and inspections of child care facilities, specialized childcare facilities for the care of mildly ill children, large family child care homes and licensure or registration of family day care homes. The site provides a Provider Search program that can identify the options, accreditations and programs being sought based on the criteria the user enters.

The options vary from live-in help to enrollment in a group facility, selecting from franchise to independent facilities to hiring an au pair or nanny or having a relative look after youngsters. For helpful ways to evaluate the best options and resources available for your family's particular needs, check out the types of care listed by the Early Learning Coalition of Hillsborough County.

Child Care Resource & Referral is a community service organization that helps parents evaluate, identify, locate and access quality childcare services available locally. A comprehensive list of providers features a wide variety of facilities categorized according to zip code. There's even a checklist with helpful information about what to look for when going through the selection process.

One popular resource for after school programs for children, kindergarteners through fifth graders, are those offered throughout Hillsborough County by the Tampa Metropolitan Area YMCA. Locations vary from public schools to select Y sites.

Tampa...with Tots

With two kids in tow, we're always on the lookout for nearby family-friendly entertainment. In addition to our favorite destinations listed below, we also check out game schedules for the Rays, Buccaneers, and Lightning, as well as shows and concerts at the **Straz Center** and the **Amalie Arena.**

Busch Gardens

This sprawling amusement park is a zoo, waterpark (Adventure Island), and roller coaster destination, all rolled into one. Sesame Street of Safari Fun and the Bird Gardens are perfect for our toddler, while our older child enjoys the thrill of the bigger rides. Busch Gardens is open 365 days a year, so we know it's always an entertainment option.

10165 N. McKinley Drive,
www.seaworldparks.com/buschgardens-tampa

Glazer Children's Museum

Perfect for a rainy day, Glazer Children's Museum has seventeen permanent, interactive exhibits, plus a variety of special events. My little one's favorite play areas include KidsPort (a giant water table) and the pretend grocery store. Big sister enjoys creating masterpieces in the Art Lab, as well as climbing Water's Journey, a 35' foot tall structure.

110 W. Gasparilla Plaza
www.glazermuseum.org

Cristin Bishara

Caladesi Island

We love a day at the beach! Only accessible by boat, Caladesi Island is a short ferry ride from Honeymoon Island State Park. Known for its pristine, soft, white sand, the island also has a three-mile nature trail, as well as a kayak route through the mangroves and bay. We try to save time for a stop in nearby quaint, **historic Dunedin** for dinner before heading home.

www.floridastateparks.org/caladesiisland

Lowry Park Zoo

Rated the best zoo in the U.S. by *Parents Magazine*, Lowry Park is home to more than 1,500 animals, located on 56 acres. With all the usual inhabitants (elephants, zebras, tigers, chimps, and giraffes), our kids enjoy the petting and feeding opportunities, the safari ride, as well as the free-flight aviaries, where exotic birds land on you to eat nectar out of a cup. There are also exhibits that feature Florida animals, such as bobcats, stingrays, and manatees.

1101 W. Sligh Avenue
www.lowryparkzoo.com

The Florida Aquarium

Playful otters and pink roseate spoonbills along the Wetlands Trail are always first on our to-see list. Our kids also love Penguin Point, and during our last visit, we went behind the scenes to pet the penguins. There are daily wild dolphin cruises, and if you're 15 or older, and you are a certified SCUBA diver, you can swim with the aquarium's sharks! Directly behind the aquarium is a small water park, so pack a bathing suit and towel, and an extra change of clothes. Parents can enjoy the cantina bar while their children splash around.

701 Channelside Drive
www.flaquarium.org

MOSI

The Museum of Science and Industry is home to an IMAX® theater, which features stunning documentaries about a variety of natural wonders such as great white sharks, U.S. national parks, and Earth viewed from space. The MOSI property also includes interactive science exhibits, a butterfly garden, the Saunders Planetarium, and a zip line. Brave, big kids can ride a bike along a wire cable, which is suspended 30 feet above the ground. Our favorite activities at the MOSI are special and seasonal events, such as the annual Festival of Chocolate.

4801 E. Fowler Avenue
www.mosi.org

Dinosaur World

East of Tampa in Plant City, you'll find a massive T. rex waiting to usher you into its prehistoric world. Among the park's lush greenery more than 200 life-sized dinos reside, including Brachiosaurus, Triceratops, Pterodactyl, and Stegosaurus. Kids can play the part of paleontologists and sift through sand searching for fossils. There are two playgrounds, and in the property's museum, you'll discover real dinosaur eggs, raptor claws, and mammoth teeth. Admission rates are quite reasonable, but bring your own picnic lunch, since there are no on-site restaurants.

5145 Harvey Tew Road, Plant City
www.dinosaurworld.com/dinosaur_world_plant_city_florida

Patel Conservatory

Channel your kids' endless creative energy at the Patel Conservatory, a comprehensive arts learning center in downtown Tampa. Part of the Straz Center for the Performing Arts, the Conservatory offers classes for kids pre-K and older. Sign up for ballet, hip-hop, tap, jazz, acting, musical theater, storytelling, violin, vocal arts, or a rock star retreat. Private lessons are available, and summer programs will keep your vacation days filled with artistic fun, too.

1010 North W.C. MacInnes Place
www.patelconservatory.org

Clearwater Marine Aquarium

Home of Winter and Hope, the stars of the Dolphin Tale movies, the Clearwater Aquarium is only about 30 minutes west of the Tampa International Airport. While first and foremost a marine wildlife rehabilitation facility, the aquarium is also a permanent home for animals that cannot be released back into the wild. Book in advance to go behind the scenes, or become a dolphin trainer for a day.

249 Windward Passage, Clearwater
www.seewinter.com

Cristin Bishara lives in Tampa with her husband and two girls. She is the author of Relativity, a young adult novel published by Bloomsbury. It's available in both print and eBook versions on Amazon.com

Public and Private Schools

The Hillsborough County School District consistently ranks among the 10 largest school districts in the country, based on enrollment. Private schools are abundant throughout the county which means parents will have options that can include church-affiliated facilities and non-denominational schools.

A comprehensive list of public and private Hillsborough County schools for children ranging from pre-kindergarten to college and university levels can be one good starting point for getting a feel for the various types and great geographic range of educational facilities available in this community.

Bigger can mean better so be sure to consider what the public school system offers when factoring in your family's educational options.

Noteworthy accomplishments such as leading the state in generating the most National Merit Semifinalists and boasting the nation's second best community college/technical center in the country, Erwin Technical Center, are among some of the standout accomplishments listed among the Hillsborough County School District's "points of pride" in 2014.

Henry B. Plant High School opened in 1927 and is named for railroad and hotel tycoon Henry B. Plant

In addition to more traditional public schools typically offering comprehensive academic missions, Hillsborough County's school system also encompasses magnet schools specializing in theme-based, technology advanced curricula for elementary, middle and high school students. The mix of academics with the selected specialized focus can represent a vigorous, rigorous program that is not necessarily suitable for all students.

For information about enrollment and tuition at private schools, the Tampa Bay Business Journal has compiled a list of 50 schools that reported the largest enrollments as of fall 2015. Tuitions ranged from several thousand dollars per year to just above $20,000 annually.

Many private schools offer pre-kindergarten programs but enrollments may be limited so visiting the campuses to meet with faculty and staff, taking time to observe youngsters in various educational environments and talking to other parents about their experiences is a process that can take time and should be done early enough to meet whatever the enrollment deadline may be.

Want to see how a particular school rates or compares with other comparable educational facilities? There is a rating system for all public schools, from preschools to high schools, as well as private and charter schools located in Hillsborough County.

Tampa Public or Charter Schools
Top Ranking from 8 to 10 out of 10

Elementary

- Bryant Elementary School
- Chiles Elementary School
- Coleman Middle School
- Gorrie Elementary School
- Mabry Elementary School
- Mitchell Elementary School
- Roosevelt Elementary School
- Tinker Elementary School
- Clark Elementary School
- West Chase Elementary School
- Chiles Elementary School
- Pride Elementary School
- Bryant Elementary School

Middle Schools

- Coleman Middle School
- Williams Middle Magnet School
- Wilson Middle School
- Farnell Middle School
- Roland Park K-8 Magnet Middle School
- Horizon Charter School of Tampa
- Mount Pleasant Standard Base Middle School

- Turner Elementary School (PK-8)
- Channelside Academy Middle School
- Benito Middle School

High Schools

- Plant High School
- Brooks Debartolo Collegiate High School
- Sickles High School

Source: GreatSchools.org

After School Educational Activities

Whether you are seeking after school activities including ways to cultivate children's creative tendencies beyond the classroom or just want to work more athletic endeavors into their weekly schedules, there are plenty of resources exist to address those needs.

For a more creative approach to learning, above and beyond the traditional pillars of reading, writing and arithmetic, families may choose from a wide variety of performing arts training programs offered through the Patel Conservatory, a facility affiliated with the David A. Straz Jr., Center for the Performing Arts. The three-story, 45,000-square-foot center offers more than 100 classes in dance, theater and music for children, ages 2 and up. The schedule presents an entertaining mix of classes and summer camp programs that can help develop skills in a child that will serve them well throughout life. The kids don't get to have all of the fun. There are classes open to adults as well.

Have a future gymnast in the family or someone who thinks they can dance? The Tampa Parks and Recreation Department coordinates competitive and recreational gymnastics and dance programs for energetic youths ages 1–17.

For those who want sports activities beyond those available through individual schools, please note that Hillsborough County is a hub for youth sports leagues. Offerings include baseball, cheerleading, football, flag football, soccer and softball leagues. Make your picks from youth sports programs offered at 59 publicly owned athletic facilities countywide.

A franchise youth sports league based in Tampa offers leagues, camps and clinics for boys and girls ages 3–17. The fastest growing youth sports organization of its kind in the U.S., i9 Sports provides a full schedule of popular sports for children of all levels and so they can participate without tryouts or drafts, focusing more on the fun and camaraderie of team sports rather than keeping score and being fiercely competitive.

Day camps and specialty camps offered through the Hillsborough County Parks, Recreation and Conservation Department are also available June – August for youngsters ages 5–17 as well as for special needs participants ages 5–22. Fees vary according to the camp, ranging from day rates to multi-week enrollments, and income-based discounts are available.

Lowry Park Zoo is one of the local attractions that offers special programs for children during the summer months. Photo courtesy of Dave Parkinson

Many of the area's attractions, arts facilities and even retail centers are increasingly creating fun ways for youngsters to spend their school breaks. Those can range from photography classes and cooking lessons to learning how to make movies and even enjoying animal encounters offered by Lowry Park Zoo and AquaCamp aquatic adventures available at the Florida Aquarium. Check with individual museums, organizations like the Tampa YMCA or media outlets like Tampa Bay Parenting Magazine for calendars and schedules.

Higher Education: College and Beyond

Whether you are interested in pursuing a four-year degree, learning a new trade or staying competitive in your field by furthering your education, you can make that, and more, happen here. Major universities, colleges, trade and technical schools as well as graduate schools and highly regarded law, medical and MBA programs serve students of all ages and all nationalities.

University of South Florida

The University of South Florida (USF) is based right here in Tampa, despite what its name might imply. The main Tampa campus is joined by two other West Coast accredited institutions, USF St. Petersburg and USF Sarasota-Manatee. With an enrollment topping 47,000 students, USF ranks as one of the largest public universities in the U.S.

The history of USF is filled with groundbreaking achievements that have furthered its educational mission and enhanced its reputation as a global research university. Highlights of its milestones and major accomplishments are too lengthy to list here but can be reviewed on a web page appropriately named "Points of Pride."

USF has come a long way from its infancy as a commuter school with no high profile sports programs and little more than basic educational offerings to draw students to campus. Currently there are more than 600 recognized student organizations affiliated with the North Tampa campus. Not only is there student housing but there is a selection of living spaces, ranging from traditional college dorms to suite-style halls to apartments complete with kitchens.

Founded in 1956, USF was at that time aptly named since it was the southernmost university in Florida as well as the state's first metropolitan university. When its first classes convened Set. 26, 1960, USF became the first major state university planned, built and opened in the 20th century.

There are 17 men's and women's varsity teams competing in NCAA divisions but the one thing that USF lacks that still differentiates it from some of its collegiate colleagues is an on-campus football stadium. The USF Bulls football team competes at Raymond James Stadium whenever they host games.

The Tampa campus is home to USF Health, comprised of its Colleges of Medicine, Nursing, Public Health and Pharmacy. From the comparatively humble beginnings of a community medical school established in 1965, USF has emerged as a major medical center. The Morsani College of Medicine is an aggressive, progressive college that is home of one of the world's largest freestanding Alzheimer's centers and the USF Diabetes Center, which is at the forefront of diabetes and autoimmune treatment and research.

In 2012. USF established the first-of-its-kind, 90,000-square-foot Center for Advanced Medical Learning and Simulation (CAMlS) in downtown Tampa, a $38 million facility that provides training in the most advanced surgical techniques using robotics and other state-of-the-art medical devices. The impact of USF goes beyond the number of degrees it bestows on students. It is an economic generator that brings jobs to this community and provides an impact that goes far beyond the county lines.

University of Tampa

One of the area's most distinctive institutions of higher learning is also a local landmark.

The University of Tampa (UT) is readily recognizable for its Moorish and Turkish architecture and distinctive minarets, domes and cupolas that are part of the downtown Tampa landscape.

Originally built as a lavish winter resort that opened in 1891, the former 511-room Tampa Bay Hotel is now a National Historic Landmark as well as home to UT and the Henry B. Plant Museum.

The seasonal hotel remained open until 1932 when it was called into military service and used as an encampment by Colonel Teddy Roosevelt and his Rough Riders during the Spanish-American War. The hotel heirs eventually sold the grand building to the City of Tampa in 1905. What began as the Tampa Junior College in 1931 transformed into UT two years later. Today the former ritzy hotel rooms are used for offices and classes while only one wing of Plant Hall has been preserved as the Henry B. Plant Museum.

It would be 20 years before the college was accredited but its current achievements and accomplishments continue to draw praise and high marks from the likes of *The Princeton Review* and *U.S. News & World Report* particularly for UT's Sykes Business College.

The picturesque, private, co-educational university serves more than 7,200 undergraduate and graduate students from across the U.S. and from around the world and has grown to occupy more than 100-acres offering a lovely, riverfront setting for its 58-building campus. While it may seem students are drawn here for the Florida weather and casual lifestyle, UT is home to serious scholarship. UT's top 10 undergraduate majors are: international business, biology, psychology, management, nursing, marine science, sport management, communication, criminology and finance.

This historic campus' proximity to downtown's business sector and cultural hub has been a boon to students seeking internships or volunteer opportunities that can enhance their opportunities for future, full time employment.

The university's NCAA Division II team rosters include a lively mix of sports for both men and women, including cross-country, golf, lacrosse, swimming, soccer, basketball and track. In addition crew, softball, tennis and volleyball are available to women and baseball for men.

Stetson University College of Law

The Tampa Law Center of Stetson University College of Law owes its existence to a public-private partnership, the first venture of its kind in Florida. The three-story Mediterranean-style building located on the outskirts of downtown Tampa is home to the Tampa branch of Florida's Second District Court of Appeal as well as a satellite campus offering evening classes. Founded in 1900 as Florida's first law school, Stetson moved from DeLand to Gulfport, a small community adjacent to St. Petersburg, in 1954.

Among Stetson's noteworthy accomplishments are top marks received from *U.S. News & World Report* for trial advocacy and legal writing and its distinction as the first Florida law school to require pro bono service by students and faculty.

The Tampa campus of Stetson University College of Law

Hillsborough Community College

Hillsborough Community College (HCC) serves students at multiple locations through distance learning programs, and the Institute for Corporate and Continuing Education (ICCE). Class enrollments are relatively small by design to encourage interaction between students and faculty members. Founded in 1968, HCC offers courses for students seeking associate degrees in business-related fields, technical programs, health science programs, college credit certificates and postsecondary adult vocational programs.

The Dale Mabry campus, located near Raymond James Stadium, also boasts an invigorating array of student athletic programs that include baseball, basketball, softball, tennis and volleyball.

Art Institute of Tampa

The Art Institute of Tampa offers students a variety of ways to learn and earn associate degrees as well as diplomas and certificate programs specializing in design, media arts, fashion and the culinary arts. Established in 2004, it is a branch of he Miami International University of Art & Design and among more than 45 similar educational institutions found throughout North America.

The culinary program gives students real world experience at running an on-site restaurant, The Tutored Chef. They create the menu, make the meals and serve the freshly prepared dishes. Diners can even observe the kitchen crew through a large window. Hours and days of operation are limited but the restaurant is open to the public, providing a delicious dining experience for a fraction of the price that would be charged at a for-profit eating establishment.

Moving to Tampa

CHAPTER 7
OUR DIVERSIFIED ECONOMY

Doing Business in Tampa

Maybe there's something in the water that made Bass Pro Shops want to cast its line Tampa's way and expand to Brandon.

Maybe there's something in the air that convinced Copa Airlines to begin nonstop service from Tampa to its Panama City hub and Edelweiss Air to launch long distance hauls whisking passengers from Tampa to Zurich.

Passengers arrive and depart from Tampa International Airport for business as well as leisure travel.

Our Diversified Economy

Or, maybe there's just something about Tampa's well-educated, multi-lingual workforce, on-going population growth, central location and commercial shipping system that convinces major decision makers to wake up, smell the Cuban coffee and realize Tampa is very good for business.

Whatever "it" is, it's working and that means more work for more people. Tampa has a relatively strong job market in comparison to other areas of the country and its multi-faceted economy has helped the area continue to not just survive but thrive.

As of July 2016, the Tampa-St. Petersburg-Clearwater metropolitan statistical area (MRSA) had a 4.8% unemployment rate, which compares favorably with the national average of 5.1%, according to the U.S. Department of Labor.

Tampa boasts a robust hospitality industry fueled by a major theme park and a major employer in Busch Gardens, outstanding convention, trade show and conference facilities, a popular airport, a vibrant cruise ship industry and an impressive array of amateur and professional sports venues. But, don't make the mistake of thinking that Tampa is just about sun and fun.

The cruise ship Legend departs from Tampa's deep-water port.

In fact, the Tampa Hillsborough Economic Development Corp. (EDC) notes that this area is home to more than 19 corporate headquarters each generating more than $1 billion in annual revenues. Healthcare and medical technology, international trade and finance are among Tampa's major industries that are expected to keep going and growing in the years ahead.

As a designated foreign trade zone, our city can eliminate import duties from being charged on goods shipped to Tampa designated for repacking, storage or transshipment. And when it comes to moving goods, Tampa benefits from the commercial shipping facilities offered by Tampa International Airport, the CSX railway system, a network of nearby interstate and state highways and the Port Tampa Bay, the largest cargo port in Florida.

Tampa International Airport consistently ranks among the leading airports worldwide.

Innovation and technology are increasingly becoming a focal point of future local growth. The Tampa Bay area is among 23 counties collectively known as the Florida High Tech Corridor, an economic development initiative that comprises high tech companies, research institutions and industry organizations.

Tampa is also home to MacDill Air Force Base, the global headquarters of U.S. Central Command and U.S. Special Operations

MacDill Air Force Base is a vital link to global military operations.

In addition, Hillsborough County's legacy as an agricultural leader for Florida continues to rank it among the leading producers in the state.

And there's much more to come in the months and years ahead.

Highlights of what's ahead and happening include:

Global internet voice communications firm 3CX is expanding its operations in the United States, with a new office in Tampa. The Tampa office will include sales, technical and educational support for clients. 3CX has 50,000 customers worldwide.

USAA, a financial services company, plans to add up to 1,215 jobs by 2019 when a new 420,000-square-foot, $164 million facility opens in Brandon

HealthPlan Services, headquartered in Tampa, plans to expand by 1,000 jobs over the next few years

Amazon is building distribution centers in Ruskin, located east of Tampa, and Lakeland, which is between Tampa and Orlando, which will collectively add about 1,000 jobs.

Bristol-Myers Squibb, a global biopharmaceutical firm, opened a North America Capability Center near Tampa International Airport in 2014 that added nearly 600 jobs by 2017

James Hardie, a global Ireland-based manufacturer of fiber cement siding, plans to invest $80 million to expand its Plant City operations and create 100 new jobs by 2015.

The Tampa Bay Partnership compiles information about the leading industries and employers within a multi-county area encompassing Hillsborough, Pinellas, Polk, Pasco, Citrus, Sarasota and Manatee counties. Collectively, the 50 public and private companies listed each employed more than 1,000 people in 2013.

The Greater Tampa Chamber of Commerce characterizes the current business climate as follows:

"The depth and diversity of our regional business community led to significant growth in industries defined by innovation and technology. These industries include financial and shared services, life sciences, defense and security, manufacturing, and agribusiness. The area also has firms specializing in medical devices, high tech electronics and instruments, logistics and distribution, homeland security and defense, and port/maritime. Diversification of services has been key to the success and vitality of the local economy."

Tampa Bay Economic Climate

Tampa Bay continues to serve as a top destination for both residents and visitors. It's no surprise why *Money Magazine* named us the #1 City in the Southeast, with the lowest cost of living in Florida and of all major metros in the southeast, a mild climate, and year-round outdoor recreational and cultural activities.

The Tampa Bay area offers best-in-class health care, exceptional education options, and entertainment and cultural amenities that fit anyone's tastes. Not only are we home to the best beaches in the world, but our rivers, lakes, nature trails, and parks offer additional opportunities for exploring the area's natural beauty.

We're home to four professional sports teams as well as spring training for several Major-League Baseball teams, and we also host the nation's premier athletic events, including the Super

Bowl, the PGA Tour, and the College Football Playoff National Championship. You'll also find award-winning museums and attractions, along with some of the top entertainment venues in the country that host the biggest names in music, comedy, and the performing arts.

We are one of the best places in America to do business, offering affordability, accessibility, and an unwavering commitment to corporate success.

KPMG ranked Tampa as the #3 Most Cost-Friendly Business Location among Large U.S. Cities in 2016.

Here, you'll find a competitive environment and the support businesses need to grow and thrive, as well as major economic assets such as Port Tampa Bay, Tampa International Airport, and MacDill Air Force Base.

We provide the critical connectivity you need to succeed in the global business community.

A top ranked airport, Tampa International Airport (TPA) offers non-stop flights to over 80 domestic and international destinations, with recent route expansions adding direct access to Frankfurt, Havana, and Panama City. Serving approximately 18.5 million people each year, TPA ranks among the top North American aviation facilities and is routinely named one of the "most-loved" airports in the world.

At 5,000 acres, Port Tampa Bay is the largest and most diverse seaport in Florida. Port Tampa Bay is also the nation's closest deep-water gateway to the Panama Canal, providing unparalleled access to Latin American and Asian markets. Interstates 4, 75, and 275 also link the region to 33 million consumers in major U.S. cities, all within an eight-hour drive.

Tampa Bay is home to a talented workforce trained in the skills companies need today, as well as students prepared for the jobs of tomorrow.

The Tampa metro area is a Top 20 market and the population center of an eight-county region. More than 4.2 million residents and an active labor force of nearly 2 million ensure an abundance of qualified candidates to fulfill employer demand.

Florida has the top talent pipeline in the country, bolstered by a state college and university system that introduces over 165,000 new graduates to the workforce each year. Tampa Bay is home to nearly 80 colleges, universities, and technical schools, including the University of South Florida (USF), one of the country's largest public universities, with more than 48,000 students.

Retention rates for state and local universities continue to rise. According to data from LinkedIn, 62 percent of alumni from the state university system stay within Florida. These rates are even better in Tampa. With respect to USF grads, 66 percent of alumni stay in Florida and 47 percent stay within the Tampa region.

We enjoy low labor costs, favorable tax policies, no personal income tax, and stable, pro-business leadership.

Locally, collaboration between government and industry has resulted in effective development practices, expedited permitting, and a streamlined regulatory process. With these systems and relationships in place, our community is an ideal place to start, grow, and succeed in business.

In the past five years, 129 companies have selected Hillsborough County for an expansion or relocation, creating nearly 17,500 new jobs and more than $1.1 billion in capital investment.

Currently, the Tampa metropolitan area leads the state of Florida in job demand, making it an ideal place in which to find a new position. We are also home to some of the most recognized names in business, including Bristol-Myers Squibb, Morgan Stanley, Citi, The Depository Trust & Clearing Corporation, Willis Towers Watson, USAA, and Amazon.

In Hillsborough County and the cities of Tampa, Plant City, and Temple Terrace, your potential is limited only by your imagination.

It's your move. Make it Tampa.

Craig J. Richard, CEcD
President and CEO
Tampa Hillsborough Economic Development Corporation

Craig Richard

CHAPTER 8

FITTING IN AND FINDING OUT

Like most Southern cities, Tampa knows how to be hospitable. But newcomers may find it takes a little time, and effort, to feel really at home here.

Growing up locally has its advantages in terms of getting to know some of the more well-established families who have called Tampa home for generations and whose names are immortalized on city street signs, public schools and even high-rise office buildings.

Breaking into those circles may seem a bit daunting at first, but there are many ways to connect with community leaders and power brokers.

Finding common bonds, discovering mutual friends or getting to know those seated around you at Tampa Opera, during Tampa Bay Buccaneer football games or while enjoying Florida Orchestra concerts, can help you quickly create a new network of personal and professional contacts.

No matter when you graduated from college or how long it has been since you set foot on your university campus, check with your alma mater, or do an online search, to locate where and when alumni organizations may be gathering locally.

Who you know can be helpful in terms of getting a fast pass into some of the more exclusive golf and country clubs, membership-based organizations and long-established social group like Ye Mystic Krewe of Gasparilla, whose male members participate in numerous community and charity events but who also help put on Tampa's annual all-day, pirate-themed invasion and parade, Gasparilla.

Volunteer Opportunities

Find a cause you want to support and you are likely to find not only how to make a difference but also a great way to make new friends.

Volunteering is an ideal way to combine your particular passion with discovering other like-minded individuals. Government agencies, community organizations and major events may provide excellent opportunities to get to meet people while also providing a helping hand.

Love helping animals? You can help wash and groom rescues, foster them at your home or provide social contact to help calm a fearful animal by taking it for a walk. Hillsborough County's Animal Services provides a list of volunteers activities and ways to help.

Metropolitan Ministries supports poor and homeless families from a four-county area. Volunteers are vital to the organization, especially during times when large donations of food are dropped off, or during holidays, like Thanksgiving, when extra help is needed preparing and serving meals. But there are on-going volunteer needs throughout the year as well.

Keep Tampa Bay Beautiful organizes community clean-ups, beautification and restoration projects that can be beneficial, and fun, for all ages. Annual events include the Great American Cleanup in April and the Hillsborough River & Coastal Cleanup each September.

Arts and cultural events and programs rely heavily on volunteers for a variety of tasks that can range from marketing assistance, staffing information tables or helping with anything from set-building for stage productions to ushering at performances. For a sample of those arts-related opportunities, check out the Volunteers Needed section of the Hillsborough County Arts Council website.

High profile groups and organizations with local chapters or offices include Habitat for Humanity, an organization that helps first-time homebuyers and families access affordable housing. Big Brothers Big Sisters of Tampa Bay welcomes volunteers of all ages, and from all walks of life, who want to provide friendship, support and stability to help make a difference in the life of a child.

Major fundraising events crowd the social calendars of lots of residents throughout the year. These can be excellent events that allow you to get involved and get acquainted for the cost of a ticket or the price for a place at the table.

Some are celebrity-studded like the DeBartolo Family Foundation All Star Charity Gala that features famous athletes, musicians and chefs. Its mission is to "provide leadership and financial resources to extraordinary organizations and individuals to improve the community."

The Magnolia Ball is another top-tier, fundraising event that benefits the H. Lee Moffitt Cancer Center. This yearly event has raised millions of dollars for patient care, research and education.

Pavilion, Tampa Museum of Art's premier black tie event, provides funding for exhibitions and educational programs presented by the museum.

Pavilion at Tampa Museum of Art

If getting gussied up for a gala isn't your thing, there's always the Cattle Barons' Ball that benefits the American Cancer Society. Think boots, Stetsons, and big belt buckles rather than tuxedos and evening gowns.

Or consider local golf tournaments, running or walking events or other engaging ways to support a cause and be part of a group, like the Miles for Moffitt races held at the University of South Florida that raises money for research programs.

Miles for Moffitt annual racing event held at the University of South Florida

The Tampa Bay Times tackles the monumental task of creating a society datebook each year that can help ensure you keep all of these important dates straight. It's a comprehensive list of what's happening and who's entertaining at these high profile soirees.

After all of the fundraising, maybe you just need time for some fun.

There are plenty of ways to enjoy all types of activities that can even more enjoyable with others. Meet up groups can provide fun ways to explore the area while also meeting new people. Or sharing common ground, like an interest in environmental concerns or ecological issues, could be a great motivation for checking out the Sierra Club Tampa Bay or the Tampa Audubon Society.

Of course, one of the easiest ways to meet others may be during your daily or weekly routines, whether they take you to your children's school, the church, temple or place of worship of your choice, the dog park or the neighborhood community center.

Local Media

The multi-county area that includes Hillsborough and Pinellas counties ranks among the Top 20 media markets nationwide. In addition, the Tampa Bay area remains one of the few remaining markets served by two daily newspapers in the U.S.

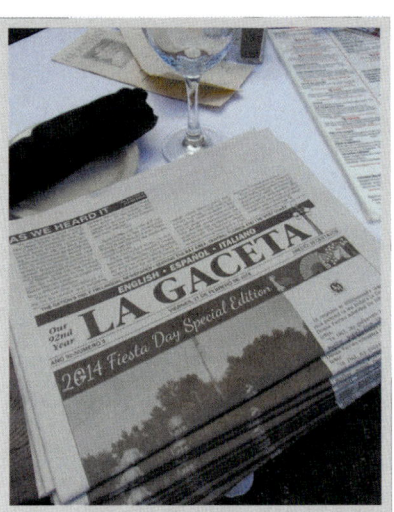

Tampa Bay's culturally and demographically diverse population is reflected in the print, broadcast and online media outlets available here. There are radio and TV formats for Spanish-speaking audiences, publications that focus on families or specialize in topics of interest to seniors and outlets targeting members of LGBT (lesbian, gay, bisexual and transgender) communities. Regional magazines published locally focus on fashion, dining, entertainment, high-end real estate and lifestyle topics.

La Gaceta Newspaper **is a weekly publication that features three languages, English, Spanish and Italian**

The market's two daily newspapers merged in 2016 into the *Tampa Bay Times*. The *Tampa Bay Times* also publishes a free Monday-Friday paper called TBT that covers current events along with entertainment, food, fashion, sports and celebrity news.

Fitting In and Finding Out

Business Publications

Florida Trend Magazine is a monthly statewide publication with articles about business leaders, major industries and issues that affect companies of all types and sizes. Articles about trends, forecasts, research and development, industries from agriculture to technology plus profiles of past, present, and possibly future, business leaders are among its main topics.

Tampa Bay Business Journal is a weekly publication specializing in local business news in commercial real estate, banking and finance, retail and restaurant, health care and all types of professions from architecture and advertising to transportation and the law.

Bi-Weekly & Weekly Publications

Centro Tampa is a free Spanish language tabloid published by the *Tampa Tribune*.

Creative Loafing is a free publication focused on local politics, music, arts, entertainment, dining, the creative arts and social issues.

La Gaceta, the only tri-lingual newspaper in the U.S., prints articles about politics, local and international news, events and more in English, Spanish and Italian.

Florida Sentinel Bulletin is a bi-weekly publication featuring local news and news of interest to the African-American community.

Lifestyle Magazines

Bay Magazine is a luxury, lifestyle magazine published and distributed by the *Tampa Bay Times*.

DuPont Registry is a regional publication that features upscale homes, fashion trends, new products and upcoming entertainment, from Broadway touring productions to exhibits opening at art museums.

Edible Tampa Bay focuses on local businesses, local food sources, restaurants featuring farm-to-fork menus and other locally based enterprises ranging from the craft beer breweries to the independent markets and farmers' markets found in Tampa Bay.

South Tampa Magazine highlights businesses like fitness clubs, centers specializing in cosmetic treatments, local restaurants and bars and hair salons.

Tampa Bay Metro offers a comprehensive overview of what is happening in the community, from fundraising events and annual black tie galas to new restaurants, where to find the latest fashions and overviews of what is available locally from top medical facilities to the leading private schools.

Tampa Bay covers the arts, special events, restaurants, travel destinations and profiles of local personalities.

Lifestyles After 50 specializes in news about events, activities and programs of interest to the 50-plus crowd.

Tampa Bay Parenting is a resource for family friendly events and activities and items of interest to anyone raising young children.

Watermark Magazine specializes in subjects of interest to members of the lesbian, gay, bisexual or transgender communities ranging from legal issues to upcoming elections, to local reviews and events plus information about new businesses and legislative topics.

Local TV Stations

The Tampa Bay area is the nation's 14th-largest TV market, according to Nielsen Media Research,[4] reaching 1.78 million TV households.

WEDU (Channel 3, PBS)
WFLA (Channel 8, NBC)
WTSP (Channel 10, CBS)
WTVT (Channel 13, Fox)
WUSF (Channel 16, PBS)
WFTS (Channel 28, ABC)
WMOR (Channel 32, Ind.)
WTOG (Channel 44, The CW)
WRMD (Channel 49, Telemundo)

WFTT(Channel 50, Unimas 50)
WVEA (Channel 62, Univision)

Local cable-only stations include Bay News 9 and Bright House Sports Network (operated by Bright House Networks).

InfoMás is Tampa and Orlando's first regional network offering around-the-clock news and information all in Spanish. Channel 900—and channel 1211 and channel 1900 for InfoMás HD—offer local, national and international news along with weather, sports and special features including medical reports, political coverage and entertainment news.

A half-hour magazine program, Revista InfoMás, covers news subjects such as political issues, immigration, school issues and other matters that affect the local Hispanic community. Revista InfoMás airs Monday through Friday at 11 a.m.

Source: www.stationindex.com/tv/markets/Tampa-St.+Petersburg

Radio
Local Radio Stations - FM

WMNF- 88.5 (Non-commercial community radio/music/news/public affairs)
WYFE - 88.9 (Religious)
WUSF - 89.7 (News/music/educational public radio)
WBVM - 90.5 (Christian contemporary)
WYUU - 92.5 (Spanish)
WFLZ - 93.3 (Top 40)
WWRM - 94.9 (Adult contemporary)
WDAE - 95.3 (Sports)
WBTP - 95.7 (Hip hop)
WVVD - 96.5 (Spanish)
WFLA - 96.7 (News/talk)
WSUN - 97.1 (Alternative)
WXTB - 97.9 (Rock)
WQYK - 99.5 (Country)
WMTX - 100.7 (Hot AC)

WPOI - 101.5 (Top 40)
WFUS - 103.5 (Country)
WRBQ - 104.7 (Classic hits)
WDUV - 105.5 (Easy listening)
WXGL - 107.3 (Classic hits)

Local Radio Stations - AM

WTBN - 570 (Religious)
WGES - 680 (Spanish Christian)
WLCC - 760 (Spanish Christian)
WWBA - 820 (News/talk)
WGUL - 860 (Talk)
WTWD - 910 (Religious)
WFLA - 970 (News/talk)
WHFS - 1010 (Business News)
WHBO - 1040 (Sports)
WTIS - 1110 (Religious)
WTMP - 1150 (Hip Hop)
WHNZ - 1250 (Talk)
WQBN - 1300 (Spanish)
WTAN - 1340 (Talk)
WWMI - 1380 (Business News)
WMGG - 1470 (Talk)
WAMA -1550 (Regional Mexican)
WXRB - 1590 (Gospel music)

www.radio-locator.com/cgi-bin/locate?select=city&city=Tampa

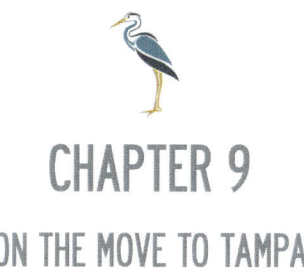

CHAPTER 9
ON THE MOVE TO TAMPA

People—and their belongings—are really on the move in the Tampa Bay area.

An analytical report released in 2014 by the Penske Truck Rental Company revealed that only Atlanta out-scored this area for one-way consumer truck rental reservations.

One caveat is attached to that conclusion. The survey included Sarasota in its Tampa Bay findings which may have helped boost Tampa's standing in the rankings.

Of course, not everyone necessarily uses Penske trucks. Another moving company that is headquartered in Tampa is College Hunks Moving that offers local, statewide and limited interstate moving options. They can pack, load, move and remove whatever you need them to tackle.

The professional moving firm has partnered with another Tampa Bay-based company that offers on-site storage. PODS provides portable storage facilities that can safely and securely keep your personal belongings on your property while your new home is being built or renovations are being completed.

That means 12-foot or 16-foot portable storage containers can be delivered directly to your location for short- or long-term storage. And, with the help of College Hunks Moving, loading or unloading these containers can be part of the deal.

Getting references and referrals for movers can be very helpful. One resource for finding reputable moving companies can be through the Better Business Bureau. Another good place to learn more about professional moving companies is the American Moving & Storage Association.

For guidelines that can help to ensure your move goes smoothly, review the "Choose the Right Moving Company" tips listed on USA.gov.

If may be helpful to do some online research to find reviews, ratings and helpful tips from others who have previously gone through the moving process. Angie's List has posted a comprehensive list of ways to prepare and plan, how to hire a moving company, common mistakes that are made and ways to estimate an approximate cost.

CONCLUSION

Welcome to Tampa, a great city that continues to thrive, thrill, surprise, delight and exceed all expectations.

Great cities are both love-able and live-able. They exude excitement and energy. They are dynamic and diverse. They are appealing and affordable. And they enable people to find their own place within the community once they find their way there.

While Tampa benefits from its central location within one of the nation's most highly populated states, it's a city that has always made its own way, created its own destiny and managed to take charge and make change for the better.

There is a lot to like here already but there is additional untapped potential as well as the city continues to develop. It's no wonder multi-national companies, major league sports, international flights, world-class medical facilities and entrepreneurial ventures are all part of the Tampa vibe.

It's always been difficult to define exactly what Tampa is simply because it doesn't fit neatly into any one niche. But it is that ability to be many things to many people that has served this city well, helping it to weather economic downturns, remain resilient while other areas suffered and successfully rebound from any setbacks, whether natural or manmade.

Look around Tampa and get a glimpse of its future. Look in any direction and you'll easily spot major roads that are being built, commercial construction projects rising from the ground and new residential developments under way.

Talk to the residents, business owners and community leaders. Walk along its sidewalks and wade along its waterfront. Enjoy a cafe con leche, a made-in-Tampa micro-brewed beer, a salad created from locally sourced, organic greens or just-caught fresh seafood.

One you get a feel for the city, and a taste for Tampa, you may very well decide that this is the place you need to be.

VALUABLE RESOURCES AND SOURCES OF INFORMATION

Local, County, State and Federal Government Agencies

City of Tampa
www.tampagov.net
(813)274-8211

City of Tampa Utilities
www.tampagov.net/dept_city_of_tampa_utilities
(813) 274-8811

City of Plant City
www.plantcitygov.com
(813) 659-4200

City of Temple Terrace
www.templeterrace.com
(813) 506-6420

Hillsborough County Government
www.hillsboroughcounty.org
(813)272-5900

Hillsborough County Clerk of the Circuit Court
www.hillsclerk.com/publicweb/home.aspx
(813)276-8100

Hillsborough County Emergency Management/
Tampa Bay Regional Planning Council
www.tampabayprepares.org
(727) 570-5151

Hillsborough County Property Appraiser
www.hcpafl.org
(813)272-6100

Hillsborough County Public Schools
www.sdhc.k12.fl.us
(813) 272-4000

Hillsborough County Supervisor of Elections
www.votehillsborough.org
(813)272-5850 (813) 744-5900

Hillsborough County Tax Collector
www.hillstax.org
(813)635-5200

Florida Department of Highway Safety and Motor Vehicles/
Hillsborough County Service Centers
www.flhsmv.gov/offices/hillsborough.html
(850)617-2000

Tampa Florida Social Security Office
www.socialsecurityofficelocation.net/tampa-florida-social-security-office-so1627
(800)772-1213

Major Medical Facilities

Tampa General Hospital
www.tgh.org
(813) 844-7000

St. Joseph's Hospital BayCare Health System
www.baycare.org/sjh
(813_ 870-4000

Tampa Shriners Hospital for Children
www.sahibshrine.org/hospitals
(813) 972-2250

H. Lee Moffitt Cancer Center & Research Institute
www.moffitt.org
(813) 745-4673

Public Transportation

HART (Hillsborough Area Regional Transit Authority)
www.gohart.org
(813) 254-4278

TECO Line Streetcar System
www.tecolinestreetcar.org
(813) 254-4278

Tampa International Airport
www.tampaairport.com
(813) 870-8700

Tampa Port Authority Cruise Terminals
www.tampaport.com/cruise.aspx
(813) 905-7678

AMTRAK
www.amtrak.com/servlet/ContentServer?pagename=am/am2Station/Station_Page&code=TPA
(800) 872-7245

Economic Development

Tampa Hillsborough Economic Development Corp.
www.tampaedc.com
(813) 218-3300

Tampa Bay Partnership
www.tampabay.org
(800) 556-9316

Tampa Bay Technology Forum
www.tbtf.org
(813) 341-8283

Hillsborough County Economic Development Initiative
www.hillsboroughcounty.org/index.aspx?NID=3600
(813) 272-6217

Small Business Development Center at the University of South Florida
www.sbdctampabay.com
(813) 905-5800

Tampa/Hillsborough County Statistical Information
www.city-data.com/city/Tampa-Florida.html

Greater Tampa Chamber of Commerce
www.tampachamber.com
(813) 228-7777

Law Enforcement

Tampa Police Department
www.tampagov.net/police
Emergencies: 911
Non-Emergencies: (813) 231-6130

Hillsborough County Sheriff's Department
www.hcso.tampa.fl.us/
Emergencies: 911
Non-Emergencies: (813) 247-8200

Utilities

Tampa Electric Co.
www.tampaelectric.com
Hillsborough County (813) 223-0800

Peoples Gas
www.peoplesgas.com
Tampa (813) 275-3700 or
1-877 TECO PGS (1-877-832-6747) TOLL FREE

Central Florida Gas
www.fpuc.com/centralfloridagasinfo
(800) 427-7712

City of Tampa Water Department
www.tampagov.net/dept_water/index.asp
(813) 274-8121

Moving to Tampa: The Un-Tourist Guide® Website

For the most up-to-date information about making the Tampa area your new home, visit the companion web site to this book:
www.MovingtoTampaGuide.com

For lists and hyperlink access to the online resources, go to:
www.MovingtoTampaGuide.com/resources

ABOUT THE AUTHOR

Newt Barrett loves the Tampa area for its affordability, its broad range of communities, its outdoor activities, its lively arts scene, and its wonderful dining choices. Tampa has all the best that Southwest Florida has to offer.

He is delighted to author the 2nd Edition of *Moving to Tampa: The Un-Tourist Guide®*. It builds on the excellent work of the 1st Edition's author Mary Lou Janson, who was unable to work on the 2nd Edition.

Newt Barrett has more than 30 years of publishing experience as both a manager and business owner.

Newt launched multimillion dollar publications in the high-tech arena for both CMP Media and Ziff-Davis.

Voyager Media, Inc. was founded in 1997 by Newt and Maxine Barrett to launch *Southwest Florida Business Magazine* and its online site, BusinessNewsNow.com. After 5 successful years, Voyager sold the magazine, which still thrives as Gulfshore Business.

Voyager Media and the Birth of *The Un-Tourist Guides*®

Like so many professionals who've had to make dozens of moves during his career, Newt often wished that there had been a comprehensive guide to the many new towns which became home to him and Maxine, often for relatively brief periods—Chicago, New York, Stamford Ct., Maryland, Boston, Cleveland, and San Francisco. Since 1997, they have made their home in the Southwest Florida, which is just big enough to have lots of amenities but not so big as to be overwhelming.

During a visit to France, they were inspired by a French book, *S'Installer a Toulouse (Make yourself at home in Toulouse)*, which offered lots of information new residents would require if they were to make a move to that city. Upon returning to the United States, research showed that there was a genuine need for books that provided essential information for new residents in small to medium-sized towns that were particularly appealing for people of all ages.

So, beginning with their then hometown they created *Moving to Naples: The Un-Tourist Guide®*, written by longtime Naples resident, Alysia Shivers. The objective of this book and those that follow is to provide new and prospective residents all information they need to make themselves at home quickly and easily—or to decide whether a particular town is right for them and their families.

The Un-Tourist Guide® Series Now Includes:

- *Moving to Naples*
- *Moving to Sarasota*
- *Moving to Tampa*
- *Moving to Greater St. Petersburg*
- *Moving to Charlotte, NC*
- *Moving to Charleston, SC*
- *Moving to Atlanta*
- *Moving to Palm Beach County*

Learn what's new and exciting about Naples on our Facebook page: www.facebook.com/MovingToTampa

Special thanks go to Susan B. Barnes for her assistance in revising and updating content for the 2nd edition of *Moving to Tampa*. She has done a superb job in helping to make this edition as current as it's possible to be.

Visit her website at www.travlingirl.com.

Made in the USA
Coppell, TX
05 December 2020